21 Resilient Women

Stories of Courage, Growth, and Transformation

21 Resilient Women

Stories of Courage, Growth, and Transformation

Compiled by Daisy Wright with

Alicia Sullivan │ Amanda-Gay Edwards │ Angella Nunes
Cassandra Edwards │ Evelyn Askelrod │ Felicia Simpson
Gloria Smith │ Jenet Dhutti-Bhopal │ Jenny Okonkwo │ Laura Tomori
Leslie Burns │ Maheeza Mohamed │ Marcela Rodriguez
Melissa Enmore │ S.S. Rich │ Shaunna-Marie Kerr │ Shirley Chisholm
Sweta Regmi │ Tanya Sinclair │ Taranum Khan

**Published by
WCS Publishers**

Wright, Daisy
21 Resilient Women: Stories of Courage, Growth, and Transformation/ Daisy Wright

ISBN 978-0-9813104-7-3 (Paperback)
ISBN 978-0-9813104-9-7 (ePub)
ISBN 978-0-9813104-8-0 (Kindle)

Book production and design by Dawn James, Publish and Promote
Book cover design by Franny Armstrong
Edited by Christine Bode
Interior Layout by Perseus Design

Printed and bound in Canada.

Note to the reader: This book is not intended to dispense psychological or therapeutic advice. The information is provided for educational and inspirational purposes only. In the event you use any of the information in this book for yourself, which is your constitutional right, the author and publisher assume no responsibility for your actions. In some chapters, names and locations have been changed to protect privacy.

Dedication

To all the women who contributed their personal stories to make this project a reality, and to everyone who will see themselves in these stories. As a part of this dedication, enjoy a poem by one of our co-authors, Taranum Khan.

Empty

Woman you are too giving!
Watch out, practice self-care
your emotional bank will soon be empty.
Is there such a thing?
How can a woman ever stop giving - loving
"You won't stop, just that you will not have it in you anymore to
give...
You can't give what you do not have"

That was eye-opening, she had never considered that as an option,
nurturing to her came as a part of her being...

Only to realize that a few years down
She felt dry, barren desert
like sand in the scorching heat

pain mixed with insult, couldn't hold her own
it hurt so bad that she peed her pants, emotionally so dry that no
tears came
while she cried, cried more like gut-churning wails, as if someone
had died

mourning loss – of being born a girl child, mostly unwanted an
apology for life
mourning the loss of a happy girlhood, mourning the loss of a
carefree youth
mourning
smiles, laughter, friendships, relationships...

mourning the daughter that she could never be
parents disapproving, disappointed
mourning limited sisterhood; challenged, unseen, lack of voice
mourning the lover who only got parts of her; a partner
unsatisfied, deprived
mourning being a lesser wife,
husband confused, hung, dejected
mourning not being an ideal mother
kids bored, resentful, cranky

One sentiment - unhappy
mourning the very existence of her being

like sand that blows around in the desert howling,
mourning its misery of not being like soil, grounded, fertile,

is soil happy?
is happy what she wants to be?

heart thirsty; mind restless
body heavy, fatigued, sleep-deprived
distraught emotionally

Face to face with the reality of an empty emotional bank

for a few moments, she felt very close to stopping
and yet could NOT stop despite her emotional bank being empty
for the woman in her refused to give up
even when not much was left to give, she pushes through,
till it's time to pass on the legacy and say goodbye ...
This piece is dedicated to conversations with women who work
hard and give without expectation, freely and fully.

Contents

Preface

There is a reason we are often advised to keep a journal and chronicle our stories – because we never know what impact our words could have on others.

In 2016, I launched the Let's GROW Project with a simple mission: to connect with 2,016 women starting with a 20.16-minute high-value coaching conversation. I wanted that one conversation to be impactful and make a difference in each woman's life. Many conversations have taken place since, even when I didn't stick to the original path.

Then 2020 happened. An unprecedented year that many of us did not envision and were not prepared for – the arrival of the Coronavirus. It continues to wreak havoc on people's lives, but amidst all this, 21 of us decided to come together and create something of a legacy with this anthology. We hope it will have a positive impact on other women, and whoever else will read it.

As you read these stories, you are encouraged to have an open mind and suspend judgment. These are stories from the heart with people putting their vulnerabilities on full display. You will experience a range of emotions: humour, sadness, joy, tragedy, triumph, disappointment, despair, courage, tenacity, resiliency and inspiration. You will read of broken marriages and strained relationships. You will meet one woman who did not give up on her dream career even after becoming paralyzed from a car accident. Another writes about the dam behind her eyeballs breaking and tears flowing uncontrollably down her cheeks after she swallowed her pride and shared her challenges with her women's group. On motherhood, another paid homage to the "thread of women supporting women, and the strength, intelligence, and empathetic spirit of the women who have helped shaped my journey." One woman pushed through with her education in a culture that didn't value 'educating girls.' She became the first one in her family to earn a degree.

Statements like "confidence gives you heels," "leap before you are ready," "finding your voice," and "rising up," are meant to encourage. Giving back is very important to many of these women. You will meet one woman who co-founded a nonprofit to assist children with their health and education. Two women founded professional networks to help their members navigate the workplace and prepare to ascend the career ladder.

In a year when social justice took centre stage, you will read stories of discrimination and racism, but you will also recognize defiance, resilience and grit amid all these challenges.

The majority of us are immigrants and our stories of struggle and survival are threads that connect us, whether it is by working two jobs to provide for the family or trying to fit into a different culture.

Finally, many of us speak openly about our faith and how it keeps us grounded when we face challenges.

You will laugh and you will cry, but most importantly, you will learn, grow, and be transformed after reading the stories of these 21 resilient women.

CHAPTER 1

My Journey of Failures, Disappointments and Triumphs

by Daisy Wright

Where it all Started

Have you been afraid to share your real story with others for fear of being judged, ridiculed, or questioned? I used to be. It was easier to talk about successes than failures, disappointments, and adversities. I hope that by sharing my story it will inspire anyone who feels 'less than,' who is questioning their self-worth, or who is struggling to take a stand on uncomfortable issues.

I was born and raised in rural Jamaica. We were poor, but we didn't know it. My siblings and I were a happy lot. My parents were subsistence farmers who grew food and vegetables for home consumption and from that small amount would share some with families in the community. We always had food to eat and clothes to wear, most of which were sewn by our mother – the very best of mothers! Church and school were priorities, and the excuse had to be good to miss attending either. At any point in our lives, we would have a cow or two, a dog, a mule, a donkey, and goats, and that was our life.

I was a high achiever, an avid reader, and a remarkable speller in elementary school. I became the Girl Spelling Bee Champion for my school and went on to compete at the Parish level (which is equivalent to Provincial). My Certificate of Achievement is still among my prized possessions.

I was one of two students awarded scholarships to attend a boarding school several miles away from home. That was a huge deal because in Jamaica during those times there were not enough high schools to accommodate every student and to get one of those highly coveted spaces, we had to pass an examination.

Up to my final year of high school, I did not know what career I wanted to pursue but decided on the exciting field of radio announcing after listening to a popular radio announcer at a career day event.

My First Brush with Failure

Although I taught in the elementary school system right out of high school, I didn't give up on my dream career. I applied at two radio stations and was delighted to be invited for an audition by one of them. It was exciting, yet nerve-wracking because the audition was going to be led by the most prominent newscaster in the country at the time, Dennis Hall. Everything was going well until I was asked to pronounce a list of words including lingerie. I pronounced it just as I thought it should be – 'ling-ger-ree.' The chuckles from behind the one-way mirror told me I had messed up, and the audition ended. It was the most embarrassing experience I had ever had, and on the long bus ride home, I was overcome with disappointment. Up to that point in my young life, I had never failed at anything, and it felt weird.

Days later, I received an invitation to the next round of auditions. I hadn't failed after all, but when I told my parents, they said it was "too glamourous a job for a girl from the country," and I should go to college instead. No amount of begging and cajoling could change their minds, and I watched my dream career go down the drain.

Years out of college, I had another major disappointment. The World Bank was visiting Jamaica to recruit candidates for administrative positions in their Washington, DC office. I scored high on the English and typing tests but failed the note-taking portion. As a free, single, and disengaged young woman, I was looking forward to a chance to live and work in the United States, and I blew it. I was devastated! I agonized over it for weeks, but the fighter in me promised myself that it was going to happen one day.

Life went on and I got married and had a daughter. On a visit to the Canadian Consulate with my friend one day, I learned that Canada was looking for skilled people like my husband Patrick and me. The adventurer in me completed the one-page questionnaire offered by the Consular officer, and when I got home, I announced to Patrick that we were moving to Canada. He stared at me in bewilderment as if I had gone crazy.

Three months later we received a formal application from the Consulate, and again, he was not excited. For him, everything must be planned. Another few months passed before I said to him, "Let us complete the application and see where it leads." This was a major risk, as we were about to give up our secure jobs to go to a country we had only heard of, but never visited. In eight months the three of us had had our permanent visas for Canada.

The Big Move

Our path to Canada took us through New York City where we intended to spend a few months with Patrick's mom. My adventuresome spirit led me to apply for a job with the United Nations because I knew they offered short-term employment. I was hired by UNIFEM, the United Nations Development Fund for Women, now known as UN Women. Joining this organization was a seminal point in my life. First, it was a manifestation of the pledge I had made to myself years ago that I was going to work with a UN organization. Second, it was an opportunity to live and work in the most racially diverse environment I had ever experienced up to that point. Third, the work that the unit was involved in was making a significant impact on the lives of women in developing countries, providing access to health care, education, entrepreneurship, and basic amenities. The realization that my poor background growing up would've been considered a luxury to the women and families UNIFEM was supporting changed my perspective on life. I learned the art of gratitude, and I started to become interested in women's issues.

A year after we arrived in New York our second child, a son, was born. One of the perks with the job was that I could sponsor a nanny for the children, so I got one from Jamaica. She looked after the children when my maternity leave ended, and Patrick moved to Canada to prepare for our arrival. Two weeks after he left, he called to say he got a job, but it was not in his field. It was in a factory. "A what?" I exclaimed. "A factory," he repeated. I couldn't believe my ears. How could a qualified engineering technician not find a job in his field? After all, the Consular officer did imply that there would be so many jobs available, we could pick and choose.

Hopes dashed, I started to have second thoughts about moving to Canada. Not only would I be giving up a great job, but I was going to miss the camaraderie I had developed with my coworkers.

Six months after Patrick left and my contract ended, I moved to Canada with the children. With my husband's factory job, we could only afford a basement apartment, and that was embarrassing. However, as disappointed and embarrassed as I was, we chose to focus on the future.

The Barriers

Four months after my arrival, I got a job with one of the major banks. After a few years, I started looking for internal growth opportunities. One job prospect left me perplexed. I was interviewed for a position in the corporate affairs office. Based on my background, experience, and exceptional performance reviews, I was confident I would get the job. When the decision was made, a less-qualified woman who had joined the company as a temp three months earlier was given the job. This was extremely disappointing, especially when my background was in public relations and I had two related certificates. I had long learned that it is more powerful to speak up than to quietly resent. After comparing notes with a South Asian woman who was also interviewed, and who had a similar background to me, I decided I was going to schedule a meeting with Human Resources to ask questions and speak my truth quietly and clearly. Their verdict was that I was 'a close second.' A close second to a woman who neither had the experience nor the education for the role? While I hesitated to think it had anything to do with race (she was white), I did come to that conclusion after I learned of prior and ongoing discrimination investigations.

Over the ensuing days, I found myself sinking deep into a black hole of self-pity and questioning my confidence and self-worth. The confidence instilled in me by my Jamaican upbringing, which said I could be anybody I wanted to be, was shaken. As much as Jamaica had, and still has, its 'colourism' issues born out of colonialism – the lighter your complexion, the more favoured you are – I grew up seeing people looking like me represented in all strata of society. It was a rude awakening to realize there could be a barrier to my career advancement, not based on my qualification, but my skin colour.

Still doubting my capability, I hired a career coach. The process helped me to regain some semblance of my former self and set me on a path to a new career. That's when I decided I could blend my background in writing and teaching and start a side hustle. I became excited about my new goal and meticulously planned an exit strategy. I settled on resume writing and began exploring teaching opportunities. Not knowing whether the colleges needed teachers, I applied to the main ones in the Greater Toronto Area (GTA) and got an opportunity at Sheridan College, a 10-minute drive from home.

Forging a New Career Path

With two side hustles, I left my full-time job. As much as it was a liberating feeling to be my own boss, the decision had a significant impact on our household income. At times, I would ask myself if I had made the right decision. By this time, we needed a second vehicle, so we got an Oldsmobile for $200. The children were quite embarrassed and didn't want their friends to see them in it. To avoid the embarrassment myself, I would park it far from the college campus so my students couldn't see that the door on the driver's side was held together by a cord, and entry was through the passenger door. The irony was when I was ready to sell it, a single mother with two young children and who was leaving an abusive relationship was willing to pay $200 for it. When I heard her story, I offered it to her for free, but she insisted on paying $100. I learned that we all go through challenges and I should not complain about my circumstances.

Although I returned to the corporate space when the salaries of part-time professors were cut, I continued with the resume writing business. As the demand for additional services grew, I enrolled in a post-graduate career development program to equip me to better serve clients. One morning, as soon as I arrived at work, I was called into the CFO's office. I sensed the layoff axe was about to fall, but I wasn't worried. I had seen the writing on the wall and was already making plans. I was offered a package, but I negotiated that they add the outplacement fee to my severance because that's what my program of study was. Soon after I left the company, I launched my business – The Wright Career Solution.

In the early years, I struggled to build the business. Sometimes my self-sabotaging voice would tell me to give up, but I pressed on. To gain visibility for the business, I would offer to speak or conduct workshops for free to a few nonprofits working with new immigrants. By then, I had written my first book, **No Canadian Experience, Eh? A career success guide for new immigrants.** One day I learned that a woman from one of these nonprofits had told her staff not to hire me for a workshop because people "won't show up." This was the same client base that would show up when I delivered the workshops for free. It was stinging, and I thought of how acceptable it was for them to engage me in uncompensated work, yet paid opportunities were given to their friends.

That realization was emotionally taxing. I experienced bouts of self-pity and questioned my capability, but sometimes there are bright spots in dark places. Although I was shunned, I never lacked for paid opportunities, including delivering the keynote to a group of 400 new immigrants.

Fast forward to 2020 when COVID-19 turned the world upside down. Not only did it lay bare the stark inequities that exist in society, but it also exposed the uncomfortable truths about racism. When racists invaded one of my Zoom webinars, spouting racist diatribe and splashing pornographic images across the screen, I was flabbergasted! Weeks later, George Floyd had his life snuffed out under the merciless knee of a white police officer. Enough was enough! While I never had a problem speaking up, I carefully considered the cost of speaking candidly about racism.

I decided that this moment was too important to think of what people might say. Whatever the consequences, I was not going to be silent, because being silent serves no one. My mantra became, "Honest conversations build bridges."

Reflections

As I reflect on my journey, I realize I have a purpose – to speak the truth and to support women. In 2016, at the height of Hillary Clinton's run for President, I launched the Let's GROW Project, an initiative initially designed to offer one coaching conversation to women. It is ironic that in the same year that marks 100 years since women received the right to vote in the US, and four years after Hillary's run, there is a Black woman of Jamaican and Indian descent, Kamala Harris, on the ticket for Vice President in the 2020 election. This is a watershed moment on different fronts, and it has motivated me to continue my work supporting women. Through the Let's GROW Project, I have built some great relationships with women on a similar path. I introduced coaching to women who never had that experience. Through a Handbag of Hope campaign, I donated handbags to a women's shelter and another nonprofit. I donated baby diapers to one other nonprofit that supports families dealing with poverty and homelessness, and this year, I have collaborated with 20 other women to bring this anthology to life.

Amidst all of this, I have written two books, earned several coaching and resume writing certifications, and spoken to hundreds of people from all walks of life, always encouraging them to never give up on their dreams. I didn't give up on one of mine! Although it's on hiatus, I did start my radio show – CareerTips2Go – on BlogTalkRadio.

Holocaust survivor Dr Edith Eger said, *"…pain, hardship, and suffering are the gifts that help us grow, and learn, and become who we are meant to be."* I have endured disappointments, failures, pain, and triumphs, but my faith has kept me grounded. And, I have been strengthened by the indomitable spirit of my late mother and all the other women I have chosen to surround myself with.

> *"Lead from where you are. No one has to tap you on the shoulder and anoint you a leader. Leadership is noticing the gap and stepping in to do something about it." -Daisy Wright*

Go Where Your Dreams Lead

Some people will tell you that you cannot make a difference in this world. Don't believe them. I have learned that you don't have to help a lot of people to make an impact. When you help one person, you are changing the world one person at a time, and that's powerful!

As Anita Roddick, founder of The Body Shop said, *"If you think you are too small to make an impact, trying going to bed with a mosquito."*

ABOUT THE AUTHOR

Daisy Wright is the Founder & Chief Encouragement Officer at The Wright Career Solution. She is also an award-winning career coach, who helps executives, managers, and mid-career professionals, tell their career stories, and get hired FASTER! Her services include career transition and interview coaching, executive resume and LinkedIn Profile writing. She is a certified career development practitioner, certified career management and leadership coach, and certified resume strategist. She is author of the Canadian bestseller, *No Canadian Experience, Eh? and Tell Stories, Get Hired*. Among her many awards are Alumni of Distinction recognition from Conestoga College, and Outstanding Employment Interview Strategist and Outstanding Canadian Career Leader from Career Professionals of Canada.

Daisy is a member of the International Coach Federation and Career Professionals of Canada. She is also a former part-time professor at Sheridan College, holds a BA in Public Administration from Ryerson University, and a post-graduate certificate in career development from Conestoga College.

In her spare time, Daisy works on her Let's GROW Project, a women's initiative she started in 2016.

Connect with Daisy:

LinkedIn: http://www.linkedin.com/in/daisywright
Twitter: http://twitter.com/CareerTips2Go
Instagram: http://www.instagram.com/
daisywright_careercoach
Facebook: http://www.facebook.com/daisy.wright

CHAPTER 2

A Wheel Perspective

by Amanda-Gay Edwards

I believe that we are made up of the sum of our experiences, which shape the context for how we perceive the world and those around us, but most importantly ourselves. Some of these experiences are seemingly more profound than others, capable of changing our perception of who we believe ourselves to be. Never would I have thought that at 25 years of age, while pursuing my dream, I would be in a near-fatal accident that left me paralyzed. I had no plan for my future or a clear understanding of how I would regain my independence and fulfil the dreams that were so heartbreakingly unfinished. Nevertheless, I set out on a journey of learning to overcome my fears and transform into the strong and resilient woman I am today.

On Friday, March 13, 2015, before the spring break in my first year of Physical Assistant (PA) school, my classmates and I had just finished a two-hour exam on EKGs. Although we were discussing the difficulties of the exam, we were happy to welcome this much-needed break. Of course, the word "break" was used loosely, as there were still assignments to complete and studying to be done for upcoming exams, but this Friday, we could finally get to enjoy the city. We made plans to meet at a bar on the popular U Street strip downtown, known for its eclectic restaurants, rooftop bars, and night clubs. A few of my closest friends from the program had agreed to meet at my place to head out together. We all agreed that it would be safer to order a car service to take us to our destination as we had had a drink. The application on my phone didn't offer much detail about the car that was going to pick us up, but there was a description of a silver car. I saw the silver car parked outside my apartment with the 4-ways on and approached the vehicle. I introduced myself and confirmed the driver for the rideshare company just as my friend started to enter the vehicle from the rear passenger side, and I took my seat behind the driver. As I sat down and began to pull my legs into the car, the driver took off hastily, erratically swerving and hitting on-coming cars, as well as those parked on the side. I remember pleading with the driver to stop, but before I knew it, everything went black.

When I regained consciousness, I was lying on my back on the hard concrete with my heart racing, utterly confused. There was this indescribable stillness that engulfed me as I realized that I couldn't feel or move my legs. As the realization settled in, my breathing became shallow and tears pooled in my eyes. My friend's voice, a faint whisper in the background, reassured me that it would be okay, and called an ambulance and my parents. I wavered in and out of consciousness as doctors and nurses worked diligently to understand the aetiology of my injuries. At first, I didn't understand the severity of my condition, but I saw the worry and despair in my parents' eyes. I felt the anguish in their tone, all too soothing and much quieter than I was accustomed to. It wasn't until the lead neurosurgeon on my case came to the door of my hospital room to talk to my parents, that I genuinely grasped that I was dying. The vertebrae behind my heart had shattered into many pieces and were causing compression of my spinal cord. The neurosurgeon told my parents that the surgery was risky, but was my only hope of living, and advised them to say their goodbyes and make peace. This was indeed the scariest moment of my life. With every fibre of my being, I believed that there was a purpose for my life, but I didn't know if I would make it.

The first few days after awaking in the ICU after my nine-hour spinal neurosurgery was nothing short of a miracle. The level of my injury was just on the cusp of rendering me a quadriplegic. I was repeatedly sedated after waking up numerous times attempting to free myself from the intubation tube, stubbornly wanting to prove I could breathe on my own, despite my lungs still adjusting from the anaesthesia. Within two weeks, I began to breathe on my own, transition to solid food, and regain movement of my arms, and made my way out of the ICU to the main floor of the hospital. The next week and a half were some of the happiest moments for me. I was grateful and blessed to be alive because I realized how close I had come to death. How could I forget? It was echoed daily in the sombre faces of my family and friends, not to mention insomnia that ensued. The mere idea of closing my eyes was too reminiscent of death, as I was fearful that I would never wake up. Nevertheless, I became stronger, and even popular amongst the nursing staff because of my positive attitude, despite my internal struggles. So much so, that the director of the hospital and good friends with the National Rehab Hospital Spinal Cord Injury Department offered me a placement in their SCI in-patient rehab ward that had a wait time of months.

During my time in in-patient rehab, I worked hard. I woke up early to get cleaned up by the nurses, put on my neck-to-hip back brace, and ate a nutritious breakfast to fuel my days of physical therapy, occupational therapy, group therapy, and daily visits from my family and friends. The physical work to regain independence came easily. After all, I was a renowned basketball player in my high school and Amateur Athletic Union league basketball, garnering a full scholarship to play Division I basketball at one of the top Historically Black Colleges and Universities. The hardest part, however, was keeping up a positive facade. It tore me apart to see loved ones come to my room, timid with hesitation, grieving my bedridden and wheelchair-bound body. It was only when I gave them a warm smile and cracked a joke that the cloud of gloom that suffocated the room disappeared. Being around my family and friends was comforting, but so draining.

As I worked hard at self-cleaning, dressing, mobility manoeuvers, and self-propelling my wheelchair, I transferred to Lyndhurst Rehabilitation Hospital in Toronto to continue my physical and mental development. I was proud of my efforts, but I did not feel ready to leave this safe refuge and the city where I felt free. Nonetheless, at Lyndhurst, I engaged with other wheelchair-bound patients and was exposed to activities such as biking, fishing, and cooking –all things I thought I would never be able to do. Before long, I was discharged to my family home that was in the process of being renovated to fit my needs and continue out-patient therapy.

While at home, it was difficult to be positive about a full recovery. It seemed less and less possible, and I didn't know how to cope as depression crept in. I would spend the mornings crying in my full-length mirror, watching as my legs atrophied due to a lack of movement. Sure, my faith was strong, but my mind was struggling to believe the positivity that I spoke every day. I began to rely more heavily, than I care to admit, on my opioid medication that not only dulled my physical pain but the emotional pain that I didn't know how to articulate. I would have probably benefitted from therapy but coming from a Caribbean household where mental health was taboo, my family's prayers should have been enough, and in some ways they were. I longed for a change, and before I could fall into a darker abyss, I slowly began to ween myself off the narcotic medication, aspiring to regain my independence and ultimately get back on track with my career and life goals. I began to focus on the many things I could do, as opposed to the things that I once perseverated on. Those things began to seem superficial and would not have helped me to fulfil the burning purpose that was still left unrealized.

I didn't know how or when, but I knew that I was going to be a Physician Assistant. A dear friend of mine had sent me a video of a paraplegic doctor and I burst into tears as the feeling of hopelessness began to dissipate and transform into an ambitious drive. I was inspired and acquired letters from my physicians and physical therapists detailing the physical strength and mobility in my upper body. To my faculty, I advocated for reinstatement into my Physician Assistant program. I was led by faith and moved back to the United States, understanding that I had to fight and advocate for myself in person. I needed to be seen. I initially lied to my parents, stating that my position in the program was solidified, despite having no confirmation. I took the initiative, not wanting to further worry my parents, and organized the rental of an accessible apartment. I hired international movers and scheduled appointments with my program directors. By mid-November, eight months after the most traumatic experience of my life, I moved without a job prospect or confirmed acceptance back into the Physician Assistant program. But what I did have was faith and the feeling that I was destined for more.

I went on to successfully graduate from the Physician Assistant (PA) program, after sleepless nights, long days of classes and studying, all while balancing physical therapy. I never doubted my abilities to graduate, however, I was afraid that I may have come all this way just for an employer to not see beyond my physical disabilities. This thought played like a broken record in my mind. Yes, I was able to finish with a great GPA and did well on my National Certification Test, but I still had doubts that employers would give me a chance. By now, however, I was quite familiar with this rodeo of proving myself and dissolving reservations that future employers may have about my capabilities, as I had done so many times in my rotations during my PA program. I was no stranger to stares of confusion from both new colleagues and patients, as I was indeed the Physician Assistant on staff ready to treat any of their ailments with wisdom, charisma, and empathy. It is my character, resiliency, abilities, and knowledge, that made me an outstanding candidate for the position.

My first job was as a pain management PA for a large private practice with numerous locations. It was there that I honed my ability to formulate treatment plans and introduced new skills and techniques for doing exams and various types of injections that were not only accessible to me but comfortable for my patients. Unfortunately, my time there was cut short due to my need for a more permanent work visa. However, after months of waiting for the right opportunity, I was offered a position to work at a renowned medical institution as an interventional spine, physical medicine, and rehabilitation PA in the neurology department.

My journey is far from finished. I aspire to continue to grow with innovative ways to practice medicine from a physically disabled perspective and inspire other disabled health care providers. Even in the darkest of times, I can find the light that can shine and nurture growth and transformation for what may seem impossible. I will never take the time that I have worked on my purpose, or spend with family and friends, for granted. One thing that I can truly take away from these experiences, is that our passion will drive our dreams, and what is meant for us can be achieved.

ABOUT THE AUTHOR

 Amanda-Gay Edwards was born in Kingston, Jamaica, and moved to Canada at the age of three. Amanda graduated as an Ontario Scholar and was awarded the Yvonne Flakowicz Memorial Award for her success in both the visual arts and athletics. She received a full basketball scholarship to Howard University, where she graduated with a Bachelor of Science in Biology.

In 2011, Amanda worked as a research assistant with a focus on Parkinson's Disease at Georgetown Medical Center, where she went on to first co-author "Efficient Isolation of Cortical Microglia with Preserved Immunophenotype and Functionality in Murine Neonates," in the Journal of Visualized Experiments. Amanda then returned to Howard for a second Bachelor's in Health Sciences, and a Master's in Physician Assistants and was awarded the Chair of the Department Award. Amanda now works at George Washington University MFA as a Physician Assistant in Physical Medicine and Rehabilitation within the Neurology department.

CHAPTER 3

"You Got This"

by Jenet Dhutti-Bhopal

It was a hot, August evening in Jalandhar, a city I called home for almost four years after I moved back to India after studying and working in the USA. I sat in the living room with my usual cup of chai and contemplated over last minute things I needed to pack and the usual predicament around what to bring. My eyes were focused on the teacup I was drinking from, a quaint little cup with flowers etched below the rim, in what I thought was quite an intricate design. I drank from this teacup many times before however, it was different this time, it would be the last time I'd be drinking from it as I had a flight to catch from Amritsar in a few hours. My eyes began to sting, maybe from lack of sleep or because I had been attempting to control my emotions over the past few days. However, this solitary moment in the living room with the teacup was fast becoming a set-up for an emotional breakdown similar to those

that Bollywood heroines unleash as they are poised to face uncertainty in their "reel" lives. "Stop being so dramatic Jenet,"
I told myself, taking a long sip of my drink before putting the
teacup away. I tried that little bit of mental humour to mitigate
the anxiety that came with leaving a place I had called home to
move to another country and make a new home. "You've done
this before Jenet, you got this," I told myself.

I was in my early 20s when I left Manila and moved to California
to pursue post-graduate studies, eventually landing a job and making the East Bay my home for almost six years. So, yes, I had done
this before. I have always wanted to build a better life and future
for myself and my loved ones. So, I returned to the mundane task
of packing, with renewed strength to take that long plane ride to
cross far too many lands, into a new beginning and a vast horizon.

It was a warm, beautiful afternoon when I landed at Toronto
Pearson International Airport in August 2010. I was officially a
permanent resident of Canada after completing all the formali-
ties and receiving a big smile from the Canada Border Services
officer along with a "Welcome to Canada" greeting. It felt nice
to be welcomed, especially after a long flight — 19 hours and 45
minutes, to be precise. I was exhausted, awaiting my luggage, and
yearned for a hot shower. A porter approached me and asked if I
needed help with my luggage. I thanked him and said I would be
alright. I asked him if there was a Starbucks café in the arrivals
area and the man looked at me, mortified, but in a funny way.
He said, "Miss, you're in Canada, we don't do Starbucks here,
we proudly drink Tim Hortons." I gave him a puzzled look and
thought to myself, "Who and what is Tim Hortons?" He may
have read my mind as he said, "He was an ice hockey player who
opened up coffee and doughnut shops. You must try the French

Vanilla. Newcomers to Canada like it," he quipped excitedly. That interaction taught me my first lesson: Tim Hortons' coffee is a Canadian symbol – there is no other way to see it.

Two days after stepping foot on Canadian soil, I picked up my bag and placed copies of my resume in a folder and headed out to look for a job. My sister-in-law told me to rest for a few more days before job-searching, however, I was adamant to find any job right away. She took me to the mall, and I submitted my resume to a few stores and then I saw a sign by Sears seeking applicants for seasonal positions. I marched in there and asked to speak to a hiring manager. After a few minutes, a man came out and introduced himself as the store manager. He led me towards the customer service area, which was empty except for one associate, for a more private conversation. Without sounding desperate, I told him I needed a job and was willing to work in any department. He looked at my resume and said, "You're overqualified for the jobs I am hiring for, are you sure you can do retail?" "Absolutely," I replied. He was hesitant and didn't say a word for a few minutes. When he finally spoke, he said, "Jenet, I am hiring for the bed and bath section. You will be doing tasks like folding towels and bedsheets that customers leave in disarray." I knew I could get past the screening and what, at this point, felt like an interview, by articulating my soft skills. I took a moment to process what he said and then spoke about my soft skills, derived from my previous experience in the nonprofit sector. When I finished talking, he said, "Be here tomorrow at 10:00 a.m., and no sandals," pointing to my feet.

I continued applying for jobs in the nonprofit sector and within two weeks into my new job as a sales associate at Sears, I received a call from an organization in the social services sector, for an interview. Within a week, I was offered a job. It was a temporary contract position but that did not deter me from accepting it. I spoke to my manager at Sears and he was thrilled and asked if I still wanted to continue to work in retail. I gave an affirmative answer and negotiated my hours so that I could work evenings for him. I needed a second job so I could manage my rent and essentials and save too.

I have always endured, and possess strong willpower – it is a well-known fact within my circle. It is not easy to leave behind a life you have built for yourself in the comfort of your home country and with the company of your loved ones. I did it twice, once when I left Manila, my parents and siblings and this time, when I left India, my husband, and close loved ones. Then the next five months of my new life in Canada became the foundation of my determination and undying spirit.

I rented a small basement apartment in Brampton, bought a mattress, and a family friend loaned me a small television, a vintage Sony Trinitron. I cried myself to sleep a few nights, blaming the lack of sunshine for my sappy self, however, the truth is, I felt isolated and there was not a single day that I didn't miss my loved ones. I had a support system and made a few friends, but the reality is that everyone was busy in their own lives and I am not one to bother others. I survived my solitary existence by watching The Big Bang Theory and Food Network.

Having two jobs made me so busy, I was too tired to be lonely when I came home. I woke up every day at 5:30 a.m. to catch the 6:30 a.m. bus from Brampton North to take me to Brampton South and then Mississauga for work. I would then catch a bus from there at 4:30 p.m. to get to work at Sears which was in the north-west area of Toronto in Etobicoke, for a 6:00 p.m. shift, until closing. I would reach home at around 11:30 p.m. and at times, did not even feel like eating due to extreme fatigue. During the Christmas season, I would help shoppers pick gifts because, at this point, I was working in many other departments including clothing, kitchen, and briefly, the perfume section. My family and I celebrated Christmas and exchanged presents and helping customers was my way of creating that holiday spirit for myself.

I remember one very cold December night, an older lady came in looking for a present for her granddaughter who had a few kitchen items on her Christmas wish list. My manager had to signal me to remind me that we were already closed. I helped the lady to her car, came back and closed the register, dropping off the day's earnings to the customer services desk and finally cleaned my work area. As I attempted to walk briskly towards the bus stop in heavy snowfall, I fell and hurt myself in the middle of the crosswalk. A couple came out of their car to help me to my feet and walked me to the other side of the street. I missed the bus that night and as I stood there awaiting the next, I looked at my watch and realized it was late and that I'd reach home past midnight. I also checked my phone and realized I got an email from my day job, stating that I needed to cover the Oakville location due to a staff shortage. Travelling by bus from Brampton North to Mississauga was already taking two hours of my time each day, and now, "Oakville?" I thought to myself. I could not control my tears any longer and let them flow. I was physically hurt, mentally exhausted, and emotionally drained. I called a taxi and thought, it would be my treat for all that happened in the last hour. The $20 I spent on that taxi ride was perhaps the best money I spent at the time because I was home in 20 minutes instead of the usual one and a half hours. I continued crying in the taxi and the man who was driving me home, South Asian in his late 50s, noticed and asked if I was okay. I nodded while he grabbed a tissue box from one of the compartments and handed it to me. "Where are you originally from?" he asked. I told him I immigrated from India to which he smiled and said, "Myself, Rahim. I came to Canada from India also almost 20 years ago. Trust me, it'll get better." In an instant, I felt a connection with him, and I told him about my struggles with public transportation due to the distance I travelled within GTA cities. I shared with him the news about having to work at the Oakville location for a few weeks. He said, "Don't worry, I will pick you up every morning and drive you to Oakville, but you will have to figure out a way in the evening because my taxi has a GPS and my boss will ask why I keep going to the same address." I was in awe of his kindness and curious at the same time so I asked, "How would you manage that in the morning?" He said, "I will only begin work after I drop you off, so if you start at 8:30 a.m., I will clock-in after I drop you." I asked him if he was sure and he nodded in an assuring manner. That cold, snowy night, I looked out at the wintry sky and thanked God for sending an angel my way.

For the next few weeks, Rahim drove me every morning, sometimes in heavy snowfall, safely and in a timely fashion, from Brampton to Oakville. From the first trip, my fare came to about $65. He said he could negotiate, although I was hesitant since it was quite the distance. He told me, "Save your money so you can buy a car. You will need it when your husband joins you in Canada. I will take $30 from you." I reminded myself that there are good people out there and that the universe is on my side.

At this point, I quit my job at Sears since the holiday season was over and the distance between these two jobs was taking a toll on my health. My manager wished me well and quipped, "You'll do great things Jenet, I know it." On my last day, as I stepped outside after closing, I stood at the bus stop, smiling, and a few tears fell. To this day, I share these experiences with newcomers and immigrants I work with, especially youth. Endurance comes from and with experience, I always say. Do not look down on a job simply because it is out of your league. You would be surprised at how much these experiences can teach you about life and yourself. We do not reach the pinnacle of our career in one day. It is a set of staircases that need to be climbed and every step comes with a lesson that is worth keeping.

ABOUT THE AUTHOR

Jenet Dhutti-Bhopal considers herself a youth mentor and is a staunch supporter of youth advancement initiatives. A community ally, she has coordinated several government-funded youth projects in the Greater Toronto Area and continues to collaborate with community partners to help enhance youth capacity building practices. A lifelong learner, she recently completed a community leadership program to become a Diversity, Equity, and Inclusion ambassador for the Regional Diversity Roundtable. She recently became a published author, sharing a remarkable story on the importance of empowering girls.

She was born and raised in the Philippines in an Indian Punjabi household and speaks four other languages including Hindi, Punjabi, Urdu, and Tagalog (Filipino). Before moving to Canada ten years ago, she lived and worked in California, delivering and supporting various programs addressing mental health concerns in the South Asian community.

CHAPTER 4

Still, I Rise

by Tanya Sinclair

Why do air conditioners always break down on the hottest days of the year?! I feel lazy and pensive as I sit down on the side of the bed, in a pair of old denim shorts and a black Wakanda T-shirt. The temperature is 33 degrees Celsius and I'm melting. Drop by drop, sweat slowly trickles down my spine resting on the rise of my curves. The breeze from the open window swoops in bringing momentary relief and memories of times that were just as hot in other ways. I let the story lead me where it wants to go.

My journey of growth and resilience:

Phase 1: Who Do You See When You Look at Me? Run Black Girl, Run!

Phase 2: Who Do I Want to Be? Can't Stop, Won't Stop!

Phase 3: Who Am I? Rise, Queen! Find Your Voice, Find Your Tribe!

Phase 1: Who Do You See When You Look at Me? Run Black Girl, Run!

Childhood Musings

Where the heck is Superman when you need him?! As a child, I didn't understand that Superman doesn't come to rescue little 10-year-old Jamaican girls being chased by racist teens in Edmonton housing projects. Superman lived in America and far away from the Ku Klux Klan strongholds of Alberta in the 1980s. Shane and his other 13-year-old enforcers were likely the Aryan spawns of the KKK. The pack grinned as they sensed my fear and prepared to close in on me for a beating as I walked home from school. "Where do you think you're going, DARKIE?"

Apart from my best friend Marla, I was one of the only black kids in my school. My life in Edmonton was not all bad. The good days consisted of bike riding, roller skating, skiing, playing dodgeball, baseball, football, and my personal favourite, hide and seek in the dark — although I'm fairly certain that the game of hide and seek has racist beginnings linked to slavery. I was young, naïve, and new to Canada. Most of the children and teachers in my French Immersion elementary school were very nice, but not everyone.

My heart pounded and my eye swung from left to right as I tried to calculate what would be the shortest distance to sprint to my house to escape the bullies. I had only one thought in my mind. Feet don't fail me now! I didn't run fast enough the day before and they'd caught me, pushed my face down, and called me "ugly little darkie." I skinned my knees and my blood stained the beautiful, new, yellow sundress with lace trimming that my stepmother had just hand-sewn for me. I got in big trouble for messing up that dress. I couldn't let those boys catch me again!

My father and I had immigrated from Jamaica to Alberta with my stepmother. We were a poor family and lived a simple life in Edmonton Housing. Although my father worked as an accountant in Jamaica and had fought in World War II for the Canadian Armed Forces, nobody would hire him for jobs with reasonable pay in Edmonton. Even a war veteran was still just a lowly Black man only worthy of jobs of servitude in the eyes of Canadian employers. The only job that he could get was as a janitor. My dad, Kenneth Earle Latibeaudiere, worked that job with unflappable dedication, donning a crisp brown uniform, a dark brown fedora, and that special Black man swagger that showcased an internal pride as if he was the CEO of that boiler room. He took great pride in doing a job to the best of his ability. I try to embody that same commitment in my work.

I began sprinting and was already halfway to our house. I was no match for older boys in strength, but I was fast as lightning. If I could just get there fast enough, I knew my dad would be standing on the porch waiting for my arrival from school. He was there. A silent, slim, and imposing 6-feet, preparing to do the weeding in our little garden. My dad's idea of weeding involved using his machete which he held strategically to intimidate 12-year-old bullies who thought their wicked deeds went unnoticed.

Five years later, my dad died of cancer, the bullying stopped, and the racism shifted from direct slurs into a more politically correct format which I continue to see regularly throughout Canada.

Some now call it microaggressions. I call it "racism with a smile." The early phase of my life turned me into an award-winning school track star, gave me the ability to quickly read situations, and built within me an undeniable survival instinct knowing that in this country, first and foremost, "I am Black."

Phase 2: Who Do I Want to Be? Can't Stop, Won't Stop!

Career Musings

Conferences, Meetings, and Microaggressions – Oh, my!

I've worked with great bosses and HR teams, yet microaggressions continue to be a reality to contend with, especially when I attend workshops. This doesn't stop me from going to these events. I'm a learning enthusiast and knowledge is power. To demonstrate the typical microaggressions I encounter as a Black woman, here are the statements I have made when attending conferences.

Early career as a Black woman: "No, I'm not the help, but I will help you find the server to get you a spoon."

Mid-career as a Black woman: "No, I'm not the help. Is this seat taken?"

Peak career as a Black woman: "No, I'm not the help. I'm the guest speaker!"

My confidence grew as I got older, discovered my unique offerings, and realized that I can overcome the ignorance of others.

The Lunchroom

I look forward to the day when people of colour can rise and thrive in the workplace and just be themselves; no longer having to tone down our opinions, interests, passions, and knowledge to make non-racialized colleagues feel comfortable. I want to wear whatever hairstyle I choose without people staring, asking if it's mine, how much I paid or touching it. I want to eat my ackee and saltfish in the lunchroom without a colleague turning up their nose and saying, "Eww! What's that smell!!??" I think to myself, that "smell" is the aromatic blend of herbs and spices of a cherished cultural cuisine from the land of my birth, and that your salt and pepper pallet clearly can't appreciate. I usually just bite my tongue and say, "Sorry! That's my lunch," and make a hasty exit out of the lunchroom feeling annoyed and unwelcomed as my colleagues resume conversations about their weekends at their cottages which I just can't relate to. The lunchroom is an interesting space to navigate as a person of colour.

Phase 3: Who Am I? Rise, Queen! Find Your Voice, Find Your Tribe!

How I climbed the corporate ladder as a Black woman:

I attribute my success as a Black HR executive to three things: lifelong learning, working up, and being lucky enough to have encountered great bosses who valued me as a professional. My journey was not easy. As I got older and immersed myself in Black-centered volunteer work, I realized that you can't always live your corporate life making others feel comfortable at the expense of your own ongoing discomfort. Being the only one in the room comes with great responsibility and it can take years to understand how to balance your leadership with your identity as a Black person in the boardroom and the lunchroom. I think the number one thing that has helped me, is to always be a professional. I try to remain calm and clear in my intent, even when others are not. When I'm in a pinch or uncertain of what directions to take, I will sometimes say to myself, "What would Dr Jean Augustine do in this situation?" Or, "What would Oprah Winfrey say to this person?"

Lifelong Learning

I have experienced a certain level of corporate achievement in my 20-year career as an HR professional. I started my career in sales and shifted to HR after a colleague told me about the workplace tuition reimbursement program. I enrolled in night school and as a single parent, I completed various HR courses at Ryerson before transferring to Sheridan College. Working all day and then rushing home on the subway to get dinner for my son and rushing to attend my in-person classes at night, was quite a challenge. I was driven by the belief that taking night courses for two years would open career doors and enable a better life for me and my son in the future. I was right! I have always believed in the saying, "What doesn't break you, makes you stronger!" For years, I soldiered on through the ups and downs of failed relationships, piles of homework, and single parenting. If it weren't for daycare subsidy and the fact that Ryerson University offered nighttime daycare for students at a low cost, I would not have been able to complete my university courses. Later in my career, I decided to embark on completing a master's degree. I put my head back in the books and two and a half years later, I walked down the aisle as one of less than five Black graduating students out of approximately 200 graduates.

Working Up

Mid-career as an HR manager, I learned the importance of working hard and going beyond what was expected of me. Working up has been a common feature of my entire career as an HR professional. Unfortunately, along the way I picked up a bad habit and at times I would consider myself to have been a workaholic. As a Black woman in a world built on colonialism and systemic racism, I always felt compelled to work twice as hard as my counterparts just to get the same recognition, opportunities, and pay. Working up for me involved taking on stretch assignments and becoming the job title that I aspired to, before getting the job promotion. I made myself indispensable to CEOs and Directors as a key advisor. Being a caring collaborator and someone who understands struggle helps me to empathize with the challenges of others.

Great Colleagues - My Personal Board of Directors

Midway into my career, I embarked on a search for a Senior Black HR Professional to mentor me. I searched high and low but the few individuals I encountered were too busy. Rather than looking for that one perfect and available mentor, I decided to create my own, personal Board of Directors. I reached out to a few individuals of varying backgrounds and professions who were interested in me and my journey. Their variety of perspectives helped me navigate that time in my career. I was also fortunate that I reported to great bosses at every workplace who displayed ABC: they Acknowledged me, they Believed in me, and they Challenged me. I created the simple ABC concept through reflection and observation and it is something I try to duplicate myself, as a leader.

Mobilizing in the Face of Uncertainty, Adversity and Injustice.

Human Resources Networks

In 2020, while the world watched the news during the COVID-19 pandemic, I, too, was painfully socially immersed through media in the ongoing racial tensions and calls for justice renewed by the deaths of George Floyd, Breonna Taylor, Ahmaud Arbery, Regis Korchinski-Paquet, and D'Andre Campbell. I felt it was time for me to do something more within my profession.

To address the gap in diversity, support, and advancement of Blacks in the HR profession, I created Black HR Practitioners of Canada. This was personally important to me as a Black woman and creating a not-for-profit was a personal labour of love that was aligned with my passions and my desire to give back to my community. There is freedom in unity. My idea was to create a safe space for Black HR professionals to meet and connect to discuss our unique challenges safely and openly in navigating and leading HR.

At first, I personally only knew 15 HR professionals. At our first virtual meetup, we discussed diversity and self-care. Then an amazing thing happened. People kept coming online and within 10 minutes, I was shocked to find that there were 50 Black HR professionals on my screen from across Canada attending the event! Three times the number I was expecting. There were many shades of melanin faces smiling back at me on a video conference. We were all in a professional HR space where for the first time, we would not be "the only one in the room." I felt like jumping for joy! I will cherish that moment for the rest of my career.

Closing Thoughts

I feel I am now entering that butterfly stage of my life and it is a beautiful thing. I'm living my best life as a mother, grandmother, daughter, friend, partner, volunteer, and as a business leader! I am my ancestors' wildest dream. I no longer need my running shoes to run and hide. I stand tall and proud with my fist held up to the sky. With age, success, and experience, came self-confidence and the keen desire to give back and do more. Having been through all the uncertain and negative moments in my life, I realized that this Black Girl is a force to be reckoned with and not easily broken. I learned not only to survive but to thrive amidst adversity. That knowledge has given me a renewed sense of confidence that is both invigorating and liberating.

ABOUT THE AUTHOR

Born in Jamaica, Tanya Sinclair is an award-winning Human Resources Executive who provides organizations with strategic HR leadership. Tanya has served on several committees and Boards providing advocacy and policy development for Durham Regional Police Diversity Advisory Committee, Telecare Spectra Distress Centre, and Taibu Community Health Care Centre. Tanya holds a Master of Arts degree in Interdisciplinary Studies from Royal Roads University and holds the Certified Human Resources Executive along with the Distinguished HR Professional designations. In 2017, she was recognized as one of Canada's Top 25 HR professionals by Canadian HR Reporter. Tanya is a 2020 Harry Jerome Award Recipient and is the founder of Black HR Professionals of Canada. Tanya is a volleyball addict and art admirer who lives in Ontario, Canada with her partner and three children. Her leadership philosophy is: Lead, Learn, Laugh!

https://www.linkedin.com/in/tanyahr

CHAPTER 5

It Takes a Village to Raise a Mother

by Shaunna-Marie Kerr

Have you ever had an experience that changed you? A break-you-down-and-build-you-back-up with different pieces kind of experience? Maybe it started as a whisper so deep in your soul that even silence drowned it out, or a roll of thunder so loud that you can still feel the echo. However it began, the experience changed the frame of your life into a 'before' and an 'after,' sometimes with an entirely different picture coming into focus. There are several of these experiences in my life: my parents' divorce, my years working with women in the shelter system of Toronto, falling in love with my husband, and most recently my experience of becoming a mother. Regardless of how these experiences changed and shaped me, there is a constant thread through all of them that looped gently around my sorrows, embroidered my joys, and sewed itself firmly into the fabric of my life. Through everything, this thread became a core piece of who I am and how I experience the world; that thread is women supporting women.

This thread has never been more important or more present to me than when I became a mother. As I was growing a little human inside of me, my appreciation for women in general grew. I was in awe of the transformation my body underwent, and more aware than ever of the literal and figurative ways in which women grow and expand to allow growth and expansion. In the cautious early weeks and months of my pregnancy, before I could lean on friends and family, I found myself reaching out for the narratives other women had shared. Whether in print or online, I wasn't looking for information on how to have a baby, I was searching for advice and affirmation that I could become a mother.

I had always vaguely known I wanted to have a child but had never thought about what it meant to become a mother until one October day, suddenly, I was one. For clarity, my daughter was born on a humid July morning, but as certain as I am about her birthday, I am also certain that my journey as a mother began as soon as I knew I was carrying her. I dove deep into the world of "mommy-bloggers" and birth stories, reading, listening to, and watching everything I could find about this experience I was in the middle of, but that still felt so unknown. I watched pregnancy diaries of women who balanced gushing and glowing with hyperemesis gravidarum, the particularly brutal form of morning sickness, I too, had developed. I read stories written by women who were full of excitement but also full of worry and anxiety about how their bodies, careers, and relationships would change, and I permitted myself to explore my range of emotions. These women shared their stories not only because they wanted to document their challenges and insecurities, but because they wanted to light the path for others, for me.

While I was pregnant, I experienced so many acts of kindness from the women around me, from women who offered their seats on the subway to my sisters-in-law who sent care packages and hand-me-downs from my nieces and nephews. I had colleagues drop peppermints on my desk throughout the day and share invaluable information on how they prepared for maternity leave so that they were better equipped to articulate their value when they returned. In the final month of my pregnancy, my mother and sister threw me the most wonderful baby shower, which saw me surrounded by generations of women (some were mothers and others not) celebrating and sharing in community. In the grand scheme of motherhood, pregnancy is a short but important time – the ultimate sign of hope and new beginnings...

Once my daughter arrived, I again found myself reaching out to learn from other women about how to recover, how to rest, and how to embody this new role. I had a long labour followed by a difficult delivery, and I struggled to understand how I ended up having an emergency C-section after all my planning and preparation. I never battled post-partum depression, but I felt guilt and shame that I couldn't bring my daughter into the world as I had intended. I hated that the first person to hold and comfort her wasn't me and was angry that for almost the first hour of her life, I was still in surgery. For weeks after she was born, I couldn't even bring myself to say I had given birth, always specifying that she 'had been delivered' or 'was delivered by the doctor.' At night, I sought out women who shared similar experiences in online forums and social media. In the dark, quiet hours as I nursed my daughter, I consumed these words from women I had never met, telling me that I wasn't alone. When I shared these feelings, raw and unfiltered, with the women in my life, they acknowledged me, understood me, and comforted me. Like so many times before, I was again strengthened and sustained by the power of women supporting women.

Like many new mothers, I existed in those first weeks and months of motherhood feeling an interesting combination of being both indispensable and invisible. Visitors were keen to cuddle and hold my darling girl, but I wondered to some extent if they saw me too. My husband was great, but I was more tired than I've ever been, recovering from major surgery, and being so unsure of myself. On one particularly tiring day, a dear friend came to visit and when I most needed to hear it, joked that 'the baby is cute, but I'm here for you – you're my person!' I had one friend visit to talk about women's rights, politics, and our passions and 'side-hustle' plans beyond the baby bubble. I had friends visit in the middle of their workday with treats just for me, arriving with ingredients to prepare one of my favourite meals, and texting me inside jokes in the middle of the night when they knew I'd be up, all showing me that I wasn't invisible, I was loved, and I was still 'me'.

When my daughter was a month old, my husband had to attend an out-of-country family wedding for a weekend, and my sister, who never ceases to amaze me with her strength and bravery, stayed with me. As a paramedic used to night shifts, she told me that she would stay up with my fussy baby and let me get some sleep. I set an alarm for two hours from then, and as only someone truly sleep-deprived can, slept right through it for a solid four hours – the longest I had slept since I had gone into labour. When I woke up, apologizing in a panic, and asking why she hadn't woken me up, she looked up like it was the most obvious thing and said, "You needed sleep, and that's why I came." On more than one occasion my mother came over to find both my daughter and I crying. Each time, she calmed us both down and set us back on an even keel, and reminded me that I could do this, I *was* doing this, and I was doing a great job.

When my daughter was 11 months, we had been at the hospital with her after an anaphylactic allergic reaction. When we finally walked through our front door, close to midnight, I finally cried the tears I had been holding in all day. My mother-in-law, visiting from out of town, came to me and gave me the exact hug I needed while telling me everything was okay. I had spent the past seven hours desperately maintaining calm so that my daughter felt secure, and at that moment, my husband's mother recognized that I too needed a sense of security. Through my entire first year of being a mother, I not only learned how to take care of a baby, I learned that there were women in my life who would always take care of me.

Just as I had settled into my routine of "mommy and me," my maternity leave was up, and I was dropping my tiny baby (in reality, a walking, talking one-year-old) at daycare for my first day back at work. Having always prided myself on being career-focused, driven, and ambitious, I hadn't expected that returning to work would be as much of a shock to my system as it was. I wanted to jump back in, but my team had changed, there were organizational changes I was trying to catch up on, and I never quite felt like I was doing or saying the right thing. I was constantly thinking about my daughter when I was at work and thinking about work when I was with my daughter. During this transitional period, several colleagues made all the difference.

I recall one day when for the third time in as many weeks, the daycare called to tell me I had to go pick up my daughter because she had a fever. As I collected my things, I was overwhelmed with the concern I had for my daughter, but I was also frustrated and fixating on whether my colleagues would question my work ethic or my value. Silently, one colleague got up from her desk and followed me out. As the elevator arrived, she got in with me. She hugged me while I cried in frustration and softly told me that while the expectations on a mother who also worked full-time were often impossible, we would always somehow make it work. One colleague always asked how I was doing, engaging with my response to make it clear that she cared. Another shared information about all the organizational changes and helped me piece together where I fit in this new puzzle, and others held my daughter in a quiet meeting room on yet another 'sick call day' from daycare when I had a major presentation to do.

It's easy to think I'm describing a sisterhood of mothers here, working moms banding together... but most of the women in these examples did not have children of their own. Another one of the most impactful moments since I went back to work, was when I was working from home and on a conference call with an important stakeholder about to present my portfolio of work and propose areas for collaboration. My daughter started to cry, and I had to go on mute. Without missing a beat, my colleague, a woman in her twenties with no children, jumped in and out-lined my key work areas and spoke about the projects I was most excited about, giving me enough time to settle my daughter and get back into the conversation. It seems like such a small thing, but I got emotional telling friends about it later because of what it represented to me, not only in that moment but also as a larg-er symbol of female kinship and unity. I'm no less dedicated or driven than before I became a mother, but the puzzle pieces of my life have changed and the support of the women I work with has made fitting everything together, a little easier.

I hope what you take from my story is not that I am a pinnacle of reverent motherhood or the icon of 'having it all.' Instead, I hope that you see the thread of women supporting women, and the strength, intelligence, and empathetic spirit of the women who have helped shaped my journey. I had often heard the phrase, 'it takes a village to raise a child,' but since becoming a mother I've seen more truth in another saying. I've listened and learned from other women, been cared for and comforted, cheered on and championed. I've learned that it truly takes a village to raise a mother.

ABOUT THE AUTHOR

 Shaunna-Marie Kerr is motivated by her belief in human potential and resilience. Both professionally and personally, she seeks to ensure individuals have access to the tools and opportunities essential for achieving their definition of success. Shaunna-Marie recognizes the power of place and identity as determinants for access to education and employment and has worked for almost a decade in workforce development to support the economic empowerment of underrepresented groups.

https://www.linkedin.com/in/shaunna-marie-kerr-b17a9786/

CHAPTER 6

Live to Change, Change is the Name of the Game

by Marcela Rodriguez

For as long as I can remember my life has been propelled forward by an endless motion of change, as I moved from place to place and immigrated to different countries. I was born with a strong-willed personality – often labelled bossy since I was young – headstrong and stubborn. However, life has taught me that determination is, in fact, a good thing, while learning to adapt and embrace change is the name of the game.

I was five when my parents had to leave Chile, the country where they were born, where my grandparents and all our family had been born and raised for at least 100 years. I come from a large tight-knit family. My mom had 10 siblings and my dad had five, so family celebrations often meant large and numerous gatherings including uncles, aunts, first and second cousins, their spouses, and so on. I even got to meet great uncles and aunts! However, as the saying goes, in life change is the only constant. It was the mid-70s and there had been a coup d'état in Chile in 1973 which meant the country's future was uncertain and so was my family's.

Now that I think about it, I realize how brave my parents were when they decided to take our young family of four and pack our entire life into a couple of suitcases to start a new life in a new country we had never been to before. There were rumours and news that Venezuela had a stable democracy, plenty of job opportunities, and was a free, rich, prosperous oil-producing country. There, we could probably find a better life. So we moved to Venezuela, a tropical, summer-all-year-round South American country, where people were friendly and the culture was laid back – most likely due to the great tropical weather and the seaside/coastal air that travels from coast to coast.

I adapted to this new culture quickly, picked up the Venezuelan accent, and I'd say, "blended in" quite well. In a blink, I had learned and assimilated the culture, its food, and a new way of living. Arepas, pabellón, and empanadas became new and loved additions to our family menu. However, in 1983, seven years after starting our new life in Venezuela, my parents divorced. My life was shaken, drastically and dramatically, as at that time divorce wasn't as common as it is now.

After graduating from high school, I moved to Caracas, Venezuela's capital city, to pursue a bachelor's degree in Mass Communications as no university in my town offered such a program. Caracas is a big, beautiful, diverse, cosmopolitan city, but at first, adapting to big city life and embracing living on my own, was hard. I missed my family badly and often felt intimidated by Caracas. At times, I doubted whether I would ever be able to adapt to it or if I really wanted or had to go through that transition to study my program of choice. But I did. I adapted, persisted, and came to love Caracas.

I went to university and graduated with a bachelor's degree in Mass Communications with a major in Marketing/Advertising and PR. In 1993, halfway through my studies, I put university on hold for a year and went to Montreal, Canada as an international student to learn English. I had family there which made things easier. Another transition, another process of adaptation, but I did it! After a year, I returned to Venezuela and finished my five-year bachelor's degree. I graduated from university with work experience under my belt. I studied for the last two years in the evenings and worked full-time during the day to gain some work experience before graduating. I knew as a young woman that I had to work hard and diligently to advance my career.

My first job was at a prestigious packaging design agency and from there I went to work for a well-known multinational company. That opened the door to me being able to work for the best company a marketer would dream of working for in Venezuela. After a couple of years, that company was sold to a larger Latin American food company. Things were going well, I had a job I loved, was young, single, independent, and professionally successful. My future seemed bright and shiny.

However, things heated up politically and Caracas became one of the most dangerous cities in the world, so living a normal life was complicated and I had to evaluate further immigration options. I had a few options: New Zealand, Australia, Canada, or maybe going back to Chile. But I didn't want to move. My life-long friends, family, dream job, everything I had built through my almost 30 years living in Venezuela, would be left behind if I had to move somewhere else. However, every day the situation in Venezuela got worse and the need to leave the country felt more and more urgent.

In 2003, I quit my job and moved to Canada again on an International Student Visa. The visa was for a year, initially, and it would allow me to test the water and make a better-informed decision on whether Canada was the right choice for me to start a new life, this time permanently. After about six months, I realized I could picture myself living permanently in Canada and my heart knew that Canada was the place. Feeling safe, not worrying about being kidnapped, robbed, or threatened when walking on the streets, was a feeling I had lost. Seeing how welcoming Canadians are and how multicultural this country is, is something that never ceases to amaze me, even to this day.

During my first year back in Canada, my savings allowed me to pay for my living and studying expenses. However, it soon became time to find a way to generate income to help me make it until I got a response to my permanent residency application. I was able to find a few survival jobs: tutoring kids, cleaning apartments, store cashier, catering cook, kitchen assistant, and some others. It was an interesting experience to work at jobs I had never done before, as they taught me humility, resilience, adaptability, and the art of accepting with open arms opportunities as they come.

By August 2005, I hadn't heard a word about my immigration papers and my savings had dwindled. I decided to go back home to Venezuela so I could create a new Plan B and rethink what my next strategy would be. I no longer had a student visa to stay in Canada and staying illegally wasn't an option. So, back to Venezuela, it was, and at 33 years old I went back to Puerto Ordaz, the city where I grew up, to my mom's place as she had a spare room in which I could stay temporarily, as I didn't have a job and couldn't afford to live on my own.

We celebrated my 34th birthday on August 23rd that year and my best friend from Caracas came to join the celebration. It was a lovely celebration and there was something particularly special about that birthday. Contrary to my circumstances, I wasn't feeling defeated, sad, or discouraged. I knew I just had to go with the flow and get ready for a new beginning.

On Friday, September 2nd, 2005, a week and a half after my birthday celebration and not even a month after landing back in Venezuela, I got a call from the Canadian Embassy in Caracas. I picked up the phone and my heart stopped for a microsecond – they were calling to inform me that my permanent resident visa had been approved and I had my papers to go back to Canada. I couldn't trust my ears! All I had to do was make an appointment to get my Canadian permanent resident visa stamped on my passport, and then return to Canada, legally and permanently, to start a new life.

I returned to Montreal in October 2005, where I stayed with my brother and his family for a few weeks. After that, I moved to Toronto where an old friend and his family were kind and generous enough to let me stay with them until I could get myself settled and find a place I could afford so that I could live on my own.

I finally landed my first professional job in Canada in February 2006. It was at a tier-one, high-demand, global consumer goods company with very well-known and loved brands. I was over the moon and couldn't believe my luck as this was a job any market-er would die for! As a newcomer, I accepted their offer, taking a temporary step or two back in seniority, but I was cool with it. I thought I would be able to do the job with my eyes closed, and I was, however, I didn't anticipate that the job culture wouldn't fit. It wasn't the right place for me as I couldn't figure out how to make the job work for me or how to fit in. The company was going through a rough time and people were being let go every single week, so it was a very tense and toxic atmosphere. You could feel the anxiety as nobody knew who would be the next one fired. I was literally sick. Although I worked long hours and frequently on weekends, my time came. I had never lost a job before and had always been blessed to believe that I was a high performing, in-demand professional, so to be let go at my first professional Canadian job was something I wasn't prepared for. Somehow, I found the strength to get through it. Now I was back to square one once again, making lemonade with the lemons I was given. It was a bittersweet feeling because in all honesty, deep down I felt relieved to not have to go back to that office, but at the same time my self-love, self-confidence, and anything that had to do with my self-worth, had been profoundly hurt. I had to start looking for a new job, again.

In January 2007, I found a new job at a big dairy company, a great place where I worked for almost nine years. I enjoyed work-ing there every day, learned a lot and was allowed to grow and become a senior manager in my field. Life was good! I had a job I liked, a life in Canada I enjoyed and was proud of what I had overcome and accomplished. I had also started a new romantic relationship and was enjoying that time when everything seems to be just the way you dreamed it would be.

Then one day in November 2007, I went to the gym for my usual spinning class on a Tuesday at 6:30 a.m. I loved spinning classes – the music, the exercise, the cycling with my eyes closed. It was just another day there when a sharp, weird, unbearably strong pain in my brain made me stop. I had to step down off my bike and could only take a few steps before I got too dizzy to keep walking and couldn't avoid throwing up. I had no idea what was going on. The paramedics arrived and I was taken to the nearest hospital. After a couple of hours, I was told I had a brain haemorrhage. My boyfriend arrived and two good friends were in the emergency room with me when a doctor entered and asked everybody except my boyfriend to leave. He told me, "You have a small subarachnoid haemorrhage, a life-threatening type of stroke caused by bleeding into the space surrounding the brain. We don't know yet whether an emergency brain surgery is necessary or how this could evolve. You need to know that the next 24 hours are very critical to you – you may or may not make it – it all depends on how the haemorrhage evolves. You may want to call your family or whoever you need to, to make arrangements and make them aware of your situation." My boyfriend almost fainted. I was shocked but calm.

Once again, I had that familiar almost surreal feeling of being at peace and ready to embrace whatever had to happen. I remember telling myself, "God, I have lived a good life and I'm grateful for every blessing you have blessed my life with, I have no fear. Take me if you must or let me live if I still have a mission to accomplish here on earth. Whatever your will may be, I accept it." I was taken to St. Michael's hospital in Toronto and admitted to the Intensive Care Unit where I spend the following days. My brother flew from Newfoundland, my mom came from Venezuela, my aunt from Montreal also came. Days went by and frightening and complicate and risky tests were done. Finally, the haemorrhage stopped on its own, no brain surgery needed, no further complications, it healed and the same way it happened, was the same way it stopped. And God blessed me once again with the miracle of life.

My recovery took a while, it included a progressive return to many things I was used to doing "brainlessly" but what took me the longest was to get used to living without fear of it happening again. It also took me a while to realize that all this has happened to teach me a big lesson on vulnerability, gratitude and to live and give wholeheartedly.

I happily married my boyfriend in February of 2009 and he has been my husband for 11 years. That December we bought our first home and in July 2010, I got my Canadian citizenship, an honour and a privilege for which I am so proud and thankful for. In October 2010, we joyfully welcomed our first baby, a 10.6-pound baby boy and in September 2012, we welcomed our second baby, a beautiful, healthy baby girl.

We are raising two amazing kids in a melting pot of Canadian, Mexican, Chilean, and Venezuelan cultures and traditions. We speak Spanish at home and my kids have fun correcting my strong "Sofía Vergara" Latin accent. There are times when I'm still incapable of hearing any difference between theirs and mine!

It is now 2021. I have overcome many challenges, accomplished many things, and have learned to embrace life as it comes, one day at a time. After close to 20 years, I proudly and lovingly call Canada home, and I know that no matter what happens in life that adapting to change is the name of the game.

ABOUT THE AUTHOR

Chilean born, Venezuelan raised, and Canadian by choice, Marcela Rodriguez lives in Mississauga, Ontario with her husband and their two children. Marcela and her kids are on a mission to convince her husband to have a pet, ideally a dog, but they haven't succeeded yet. Marcela is an avid reader, especially about topics relating to leadership, parenting, growth and personal development, and she is always trying to find answers to her endless, "Wait, but why?" questions. She has made a career in marketing after graduating with a bachelor's degree in Mass Communications from Andres Bello University, and a master's in Marketing from IESA in Caracas, Venezuela.

CHAPTER 7

The Journey to Success is the Destination

by Laura Tomori

One of my favourite quotes is by Helen Keller and it goes like this, "Although the world is full of suffering, it is also full of the overcoming of it." This quote deeply resonates with me and I frequently remind myself of its truth when I am faced with challenges and adversity.

I grew up as the first female child in a lower-middle-class family in the city of Lagos, Nigeria, West Africa. Post-secondary education for females was not encouraged in my extended family as it was deemed a waste of resources because a woman would end up in a man's house and be cared for by their husbands. My mother told me that she had great potential but was not allowed to go to school beyond Elementary School 5 as her father thought their resources were better spent on her brothers and half-brothers. So, from a very tender age, she drummed it into my ears that post-secondary education was non-negotiable for me. She told me I had to lead the path for my siblings, especially my two younger sisters, to follow. She would frequently exempt me from house chores so that I could focus my attention on my academics.

My earliest memory of facing and overcoming a challenge was just after my last year of secondary school while trying to secure admission into Delta State University to study Mass Communication. I grew up being intrigued by the female newscasters I saw on television and wanted to be just like them. I decided that I would study Mass Communication so I could get a job on TV. I wrote the university's admissions examination in my last year of Senior Secondary at the tender age of 16. I scored above the cut-off mark to study Mass Communication. I was giddy with joy when I received my Admissions Examinations result and could not stop broadcasting my good fortune to everyone, especially my peers who still had a year to go before writing the exam. I was so sure that securing admission was going to be a breeze – after all, I had the qualifying scores. Little did I know that I was about to embark on a challenging emotional and mental journey.

I took a trip to the university town and was accompanied by my maternal uncle who lived in a town close by. We met with the admissions officer and were told that in addition to the cut-off marks, there was usually an internal screening done by the admissions committee. This was quite surprising to me as I thought scoring above the cut-off mark meant automatic admission, but I was still quite confident that I would be among those chosen. He informed us that they would usually publish three different lists of successful candidates during admissions season and that I should keep my ears to the ground to know when the list was published and to check if I was selected.

I began to make weekly trips to the university. I toured the faculty, lecture halls, and residences during one such trip. I could already see myself living and attending school. The first, second and third list of successful candidates was published in the space of one month and my name was nowhere on the list! I cannot remember how I made it back home on that last trip as my thoughts travelled in different directions and I couldn't begin to fathom what had just happened. I cried until I had no strength left.

The next day my uncle suggested we go check out my second choice which was Ambrose Alli University to study English Language and Literature. I was very discouraged as I had set my hopes on Delta State University. Moreover, the admissions season was almost over across the country and I thought they would be done with publishing their list of successful candidates. I reluctantly agreed to go with him. A friend of my uncle that knew the Head of Faculty wrote me a support letter to take to him.

We arrived at the university and asked for directions to the professor's office. When we got there, there was a long line of people waiting to see him. We waited for what felt like forever. Every hour of waiting added to my sense of panic, but I told myself that I had nothing to lose. When we finally got to meet with him, the faculty head looked through my credentials and informed me that the admissions process was closed but there was going to be a final supplementary list that would be published within the next week. He said my chances were very slim as there were lots of other equally qualified candidates.

That week of waiting was the longest in my life, but I kept a positive attitude and kept reminding myself that I did my best. On the day of the posting, I took public transport to the university town. It was a very sunny and humid day and there was a long line at the admissions office but my whole focus was on discovering my fate. Prospective students kept coming out with long faces after going in to check the posted list. My heart was racing and my palms sweaty as I waited my turn. When it was finally my turn, I went in. There were several pages of printed names posted on the wall and the names were arranged in alphabetical order. I scanned the names for my last name and as I was looking, I saw my last and first name! The world came to a standstill, I didn't know whether to cry or laugh. Excited, I ran outside. My dream of going to university had finally materialized. I couldn't wait to go home and inform my family and friends about the good news. I was going to be the first female in my family to attend post-secondary education!

Even though Mass Communication had been my first course, I later realized that English and Literature were a better choice for me because it was a much broader course of study than Mass Communication. It gave me the best of both worlds and I ended up with a more rounded education. I attended Ambrose Alli University, worked hard at my studies, and graduated with a Bachelor of Arts degree. After graduation, I secured a job in one of the banks in Nigeria and started working.

Transitioning to a career in Canada also proved to be a challenge. I landed in Canada as a Permanent Resident in late 2006 with my 14-month-old daughter and wasn't sure what to expect from the career landscape. After settling down in early 2007, I started looking into career options. A friend that I knew from back home told me about her career as an IT Business Analyst. I became intrigued and started doing online studies on the skills and role of an IT Business Analyst. The more I studied, the more interested I became, and I saw parallels and transferable skills with my role at the bank, back in Nigeria.

Friends and family told me I was aiming too high, that I didn't have Canadian experience, and that I was better off finding a less skilled job. I tried securing a less skilled job, but the hours I was offered didn't work for my family schedule as I was by myself with my daughter, who was not yet in school. I became confused about what to do but deep in my heart, I knew I wanted a career in the people side of Information Technology.

For about two months, I would get up early before my daughter woke and do my online studies. I called my Business Analyst friend on her train ride to or from work every day and would ask her questions about her role and responsibilities. We brainstormed together on how to speak to my transferable skills. After another month, I updated my resume and started applying for jobs.

I would check out company websites, Monster and Workopolis, and apply to positions that I felt suitable for. I quickly learned that a generic resume would not fly so I started updating my resume to fit the job description before applying. When I saw that I wasn't getting any calls from hiring managers or recruiters, I posted a copy of my resume on job sites and refreshed it every morning so it would come up in searches. I got invited to a few interviews which I attended but after going through several stages in the hiring process I was informed that they had decided to go with a more experienced candidate. This made me quite sad and downcast and I became very discouraged.

I wasn't sure how I would get Canadian experience if no one was willing to give me a chance. My friend would often encourage me to not give up hope, but it was difficult for me to see how I was going to find a job. At one point I decided to take a break from applying for jobs as the emotional and mental toll of the rejections became too much for me. I took two weeks off applying for jobs and took the time to do the things that bring me joy: taking long walks with my daughter and reading motivational books and articles. I slowly started ridding myself of the ways I had been internalizing the rejections.

After my break, I decided to be more strategic in my approach to job hunting. I borrowed and read interview prep books from the library and practised my interview pitch in front of a mirror. After about three weeks of doing this, I was at the mall one day when my phone rang. It was a hiring manager calling to inform me that they found my resume on a job site and were looking to fill a role in IT Quality Assurance. We spoke for a few minutes and they scheduled a face-to-face interview for the following week. I attended the interview and felt a connection. They informed me that they would get back to me in about a week as they were interviewing other candidates. I prayed to God to please let it be me and waited. This time, however, I had learned to trust and believe that what is mine will not pass me by. Exactly a week later, I opened my email and saw an offer email from them. I will never forget the sense of joy and gratitude that I felt that day.

That offer began a career in IT that has spanned over 13 years. I have had many titles ranging from Business Analyst to Business Systems Consultant to Project Team Lead, and I have been pushed outside my comfort zone. I have had successes and failures but I have also grown, and I continue to learn and grow every day.

In looking back at my personal life and career to this point, and all the adversities I have experienced and continue to face as I advance, I am reminded of a quote by Dr Maya Angelou, "You may encounter many defeats, but you must not be defeated." I also remind myself that the journey to success is the destination.

ABOUT THE AUTHOR

 Laura Tomori is a technology evangelist who helps companies achieve digital transformation by implementing technological solutions to solve business problems and facilitating business outcomes that focus on customer experience. Her expertise includes analysis of business needs, requirements gathering and documentation, automation capabilities, process mapping, data visualization, User Acceptance Testing, building relationships, and active listening, to name a few.

Laura has over 14 years' experience as a Software Tester, Business Systems Analyst, Project Team Lead, and Senior Business Consultant in the banking, insurance, consumer services, finance, and consulting sectors.

Laura's core values include making a difference and imparting knowledge to the next generation which is in line with the United Nations' Sustainable Development Goal No. 4: Quality Education. She volunteers with The Learning Partnership as a business mentor where she led one of eight team finalists for the 2018 Dragon's Nest competition. She also currently volunteers with the Spelling Bee of Canada. Her hobbies are travelling and journaling.

LinkedIn: https://www.linkedin.com/in/lauratomori/
Twitter: https://twitter.com/LauraTomori

CHAPTER 8

Jamaica, My First Love

by Felicia Simpson

I sat by the lake throwing pebbles into the water, one by one, as I often found myself doing on many of my long walks. I was reminiscing about the time I spent growing up in Jamaica and the many times I visited after making Canada my new home.

I was born and grew up in the beautiful, sunny island of Jamaica in the Caribbean. Jamaica was referred to as "The Land of Wood and Water." Surrounded by the Caribbean Sea, it's a gem boasting beautiful sandy beaches, lush mountains and vegetation, savoury food, and the best fruits you could ever experience the taste of. My favourite fruit was its sweet, yellow, juicy mango, that hung so low that we could easily reach up and pick it directly from the trees. They were so plentiful during the mango season, May to July, that you often would see trees laden with them as well as ripe ones scattered on the ground below.

I have a big family that consists of four girls and two boys. I am the youngest girl and my brother Sonny is the youngest boy. We had another sister, Norma, who, unfortunately, was killed in a soldier lorry accident years before I was born. I wish I had known her. My family was not poor, but they weren't rich either. We were born in Kingston, the capital of Jamaica where we lived in a modest house and always had dogs. My mother was my rock! I idolized her. She was the epitome of strength, compassion, and love. She was a housewife, just like a lot of mothers at that time. You would think that because she didn't go out to work that she had it easy. In fact, it was the opposite. Her life was tough. She would get up at 5:00 a.m. and make us breakfast so we could have something healthy in our stomachs to face the school day. After making breakfast and leaving it on the stove for us, she would go outside to start washing the clothes. Washing machines didn't exist back then so washing was done by hand and the sun was the dryer. My brothers' clothes would be so dirty when they got home from school that my mother had to use all her strength to scrub them clean.

Mama was my anchor. She taught me so much. Her faith in God was abounding. She would sing gospel songs while she worked. She always had her Bible with her and would travel throughout the house with a little transistor radio, listening to her songs, the news, and her daily stories. One of my fondest memories was watching her as she sat in front of the mirror, braiding her hair into two long braids, and wrapping them up neatly into a bun. She was also a seamstress and was able to produce amazing clothes.

She made stunning veils and wedding gowns with the longest trains adorned with beautiful, shiny sequins. She would sew one sequin at a time by hand, and her patience and diligence allowed her to create the most immaculate and spectacular designs.

There were many important lessons that Mama taught me but three of them influenced my life the most. The first was to always be grateful and to keep praying. She would often say, "Rest your burden on the Lord's shoulders." The next was to keep your business private. She said, "Never let your right hand know what your left hand is doing." The last thing Mama taught me, and the most important, was how to be selfless. She would sometimes go without food so that we could eat. She never complained about all the work she had to do. She was emotionally there for us and never once put herself first. Even though she loved us, she was a disciplinarian. If we were out of line, she would give you "that look" and you would know exactly what that meant! The strap was also never far away. When I look back at all the discipline she meted out, I would not have had it any other way. This type of discipline was shaping us into the types of individuals we were later to become.

I don't have a vivid recollection of my father as he left us when I was only ten years old. I know, as a young child, he used to buy us a lot of toys. I can, however, remember a little toy doggie that he bought me. It was yellow with black dots on it. It was on wheels and I used to pull it around in circles. My father was a musician and he could play the guitar very well. I remember that one of his fingers was missing the tip. I am not sure what kind of accident he had, and I don't believe I ever asked, but I always wondered about it. I also remember that he loved to drink Appleton rum, like so many men at that time. He preferred Appleton yellow and white rum. He would often come home a bit tipsy and his balance seemed to be a bit off as he struggled to come up the stairs. He was always very cheerful. Whenever anyone would say anything derogatory to him, he would just chuckle. He worked as an electrician and a salesman. I am not sure how I felt about him not being around all those years as I was growing up. My mother did a good job of acting as both mother and father and I was always so busy studying that I didn't have much time to miss that relationship. Much later, during a few of my trips to Jamaica, we did communicate and, in 1997, we all attended my brother's wedding there.

I remember every day sitting on the verandah waiting for my ride to go to school. That verandah played a significant part in my growing-up years. I spent many mornings sitting there waiting for my ride. That morning, my sister's ride came as it always did, before mine. In the back seat of the car was my sweetheart crush! As usual, he waved to me and I waved back, with a smile. Every morning it was the same routine and I looked forward to it. It prepared me for the day at school. I attended a Roman Catholic all-girls' high school. It was a strict high school run by nuns. The school uniform was all white with a blue tie and a "jippi-jappa" hat, brown shoes, and white socks. No jewellery or makeup was allowed. If ever a student decided she wanted to shorten her skirt, the nuns would embarrass her in front of her friends by pulling that hem down and she would be given a detention! Demerits and detentions were quite common. School was tough! I had to study hard. I remember "swatting" for exams and my answers to some of the questions on the exam papers were "word-for-word" out of the book. I memorized a lot of what I studied and was very disciplined and maybe a bit serious at times. I always tried to do the right thing and was mostly a positive and happy student but sometimes lacked self-confidence.

I had been accepted to high school after earning a scholarship through the Common Entrance examinations. The first time I took the exams, I received a half scholarship. A student could be accepted into high school with a half scholarship, but my mother couldn't afford to send me as she would have had to pay a portion of the tuition. I took the exams again the following year and thankfully I received the full scholarship. I was relieved and excited!

The school system consisted of four levels called Forms – 1A, 1B, 1C, 1D. I started in 1C. The following year, I did so well that I was promoted to 2B. The next year, I was promoted to 3A and stayed in the "A" stream until 5th Form, where I graduated and pursued Secretarial studies. With my grades, I should have ventured on to 6th Form but, unfortunately, my mother couldn't afford to send me. She always wanted one of us to be a nurse. Unfortunately, that didn't happen either.

David was my sweetheart crush. He was so cute, and his wave and shy smile always melted my heart. I looked forward to that smile every morning. After many mornings of this ritual, we finally met but I can't remember exactly how it happened. All I know is that I invited him to be my date at my graduation ceremony and he accepted. It was magic! We were meant for each other! He was the perfect gentleman. Our relationship grew and we began spending more time together. We were no longer waving and smiling from afar as our flirtation had blossomed into a beautiful relationship. I even ended up working at his parents' jewellery store every Saturday and I earned J$14.00 for each shift. I enjoyed working in that store and coming from a modest-income family, I was mesmerized by all the beautiful gems that surrounded me. There were diamonds, rubies and pearls, white gold, yellow gold, sterling silver, and expensive watches. I was in Fairy Land! When my birthday rolled around, David always surprised me with a piece of jewellery, a stuffed animal, and flowers. I was moved by his generosity and gentle nature. And, when he asked me to marry him, I said YES.

We got married in a small Roman Catholic Church amidst a small number of guests. When I look back at my wedding photos, I looked so young, as I was only 20 years old, and wore no makeup. As I walked up the aisle, I had mixed feelings. I didn't think I was ready for this responsibility. I felt like changing my mind and running away but didn't dare to do so.

We immigrated to Canada in 1976 when I was 21 years old. I arrived in July, so the weather was somewhat like that of Jamaica. When the fall and winter arrived, I enjoyed the cool weather and the flurries. However, when the real snow began and the cold, cold weather set in, I cried. And to make matters worse, our relationship started to go downhill. The love that I thought I felt at the beginning of our relationship had waned. Things didn't stay as rosy as they were in the beginning and within three years, I packed up and moved out, leaving a note for David. I didn't have the courage to face him. When I left, I tasted freedom and it tasted sweet! This was the beginning of the rest of my journey through life in a country without my mother and brothers. The good thing was that I still had three sisters who had immigrated to Canada earlier so I wasn't alone.

Being single in Canada proved to be exciting. I met many new people and made quite a few new friends. There was so much to do. I joined a squash club, a tennis club, went on cruises on Lake Ontario and dined at restaurants offering a variety of different dishes from all over the world. There were also activities like Caribana that brought together people from the Caribbean who live all over the world to celebrate this annual cultural event in Toronto. There were so many other events like these organized by people from other countries, so we got the opportunity to experience the culture and food from those countries.

My mother has been a great influence in my life as her lessons taught me well. Life in both Canada and Jamaica is good. I especially treasure my time spent in Jamaica because that's where my life began. And that's where I first met my friends, especially my schoolmates. There are many storms to weather, though. In Jamaica, there was a certain type of class prejudice that existed which I think still exists. I believe this stems from our slavery past. I experienced a lot of that in high school. Coming to Canada and starting afresh, also had its challenges and hurdles. It was important for me to use this experience to deal with the racism I experienced in Canada when I arrived here and during the time I have been here.

As I sat reminiscing while throwing the pebbles in the lake, I realized that it had gotten dark and it was time to go home. I stood up, looked around me and at that moment realized that you can be happy anywhere, as long as you focus on the positive and hold on to treasured memories.

ABOUT THE AUTHOR

Felicia Simpson was born in Kingston, Jamaica, but has spent most of her life in Canada. She spent over 20 years in the corporate world and holds certificates in Marketing Management and HR Management with honours from Ryerson and Sheridan College, respectively. She also holds certificates in both French and Spanish. She is a member of Toastmasters International and was recently appointed VP Membership.

Felicia is highly respected by her colleagues and friends and is known as a positive, friendly, resourceful, dedicated, hard-working, and reliable individual. She enjoys helping others and giving back to the community by volunteering at a retirement residence in Brampton, Ontario. She regularly participates in fundraising activities to support the Heart and Stroke Foundation, the Cancer Society, and other charities.

Connect with Felicia:
LinkedIn: linkedin.com/in/feliciaesimpson/

CHAPTER 9

Don't Cast Away Your Hope

by S.S. Rich

My friends laugh out loud whenever I say, "These are the colours of the flowers that I want on my wedding day!" or "This is where I'd like to go on my honeymoon."

"Don't you actually have to be dating someone?" they remind me, unsympathetically.

So what's the big deal with this, you may be thinking? There are far worse things that could happen in a lifetime. But I humbly disagree. I am recording this experience for those who have had similar experiences and never had them validated or spoken of because of shame or defeat or mockery. I am telling my story as it may be a healing balm or give courage to those voices that have been silenced. I would like our voices to become like roaring lions that propel us forward and embolden us to keep running the race that is marked for us (Hebrews 12:1-2 KJV). I want us to stop hiding our hearts because they are the entrance to our beautiful souls, minds, will, and emotions.

As I was saying, my friends laugh because I'm still single and I have not dated in over two decades. The last person I loved was secretly seeing someone else and I discovered that he was marrying this younger woman (his colleague) – who had more prestige, status and youth on her side than I did – on the day he was going to get married! His family, whom I was fond of and thought was fond of me, was too embarrassed to tell me. As I mustered the courage to ask them, I wasn't thinking of putting his mom in a difficult position, I just wanted to hear her say what I had already known in my gut to be the truth. The man I thought loved me had proposed marriage to another woman right before my eyes.

This was one of the most difficult, heart-wrenching betrayals of my life. At the time, my aunt (whom I lived with) held me, literally and figuratively, through the deep darkness of the days, months and years that lay ahead – the black, empty void of despair that I thought I would never see the other side of, but I did! There were days when I planned revenge, nights when I cried myself to sleep, and months when I slowly began to be honest with myself about the many reasons why this person would not have been a good husband or father or friend. I uncovered many truths in my candid self-reflection and inner healing, but the most profound for me was that I was too young, immature, and naïve. He was too selfish, self-absorbed, and disrespectful with his contemptuous actions and deceitful words to have been my "Mister Right!" I realized that any person that you idolize will never be the person for you. We lose our self-worth and identity when we are consumed with pleasing and compromising who we are to gain another's attention and love. Sadly, it is not the sweet, pure love that we deserve, nor will it ever be reciprocated.

The love and value that I was looking for, that we are ALL looking for, can only come from God and from the revelation that we are worthy of honour and respect as human beings. People will treat you how you allow them to treat you. If you behave as if you are their doormat, they will treat you as one, and that is how I allowed this person to treat me so many years ago because I wanted him to fill a void for me that only God could.

I asked God to help me not to repeat this mistake and to lead the way in finding a suitable partner. This has not yet come to fruition. So, I kind of understand when my friends make these nonchalant comments. They don't get it and why should they? It is my story, I am the protagonist, and God is speaking to my heart, not theirs. But their words still hurt! I feel a little smaller, a little less significant every time it happens, and recently, I've begun to feel a little less valuable to the point of secretly berating myself. I flounder, but I refuse to accept defeat.

Have you ever been there, where it seems like everybody's life seems to be moving ahead and your life seems stuck in the same place year after year, season after season? You lay in bed at night and wonder, what is my purpose here? Am I marriage material? Do I have something that I can share with others that will make a difference? The answer to all these questions is yes, yes, and yes!

Our lives matter and things that are important to us matter. We are made in God's image (Genesis 1:27) and that means we are wonderfully and fearfully made (Psalm 139:14); perfect! God made each of us with a purpose that is unique to our personality, strengths and even our weaknesses. If we have desires, God has placed those desires in us (Philippians 2:13) to be used for His glory.

Simply put, when we are truly happy, we are most powerful in our spirit and it brings God glory! If we can make one person happy on our path, it brings God glory too. Isn't that magnificent? We have that innate power within us to do something positive for other human beings every day. Sometimes we miss it because we are looking for big, grand things, but life is all about the daily grind, the mundanity of Sunday, Monday, Tuesday, Wednesday, Thursday, Friday and Saturday. Repeat. If we take time to notice, we will discover that there is so much in us we can give, but are we giving? There is a parable in the Bible that talks about Jesus giving talent and amongst three people he gave talent to, one did nothing with it. God was not pleased then, and He will not be pleased now if we are not using the talent He has already given us. Talent can represent the gift of listening, the gift of talking, the gift of laughter, the gift of sharing, and the gift of loving ourselves healthily. It doesn't have to be a grand Instagram moment, just a smile and kind words in passing can be tremendously impactful. (Matthew 25:14-30 ESV).

We can become consumed with our assignment (career), our ministry (church), our duties as momma or as a wife, and forget to balance. There must be a balance, an ebb and flow between our roles to build depth and beauty with the interwoven components of family and friends. I tell my class each year, "You may be rich, intelligent, beautiful, strong and healthy, but if you have no one to share your life with – you are poor and miserable." The same is true for each of us. People matter, having people in our lives matters, sharing life with others in meaningful ways matters, and we should never take people for granted by not giving them space to grow or our full attention when it is required.

I do have a desire to be married, and why should I be ashamed to admit it? Because I get laughed at and I'm told that I'm not doing anything about it. I'm not going after it. I am not being purposeful, strategic and aggressive enough about fulfilling this dream. Has anyone else ever experienced that? It baffles me because there isn't a reason why we shouldn't feel free to discuss it.

I have been fortunate enough to have a prayer partner for the past decade who holds my hands each week and brings that prayer request to God, with me. We've been doing this for years. When I'm weak she becomes the voice of my prayers. She encourages me, builds me up, and reminds me when my heart grows cold and despondent about God's plan for me to be married. We all need someone like that in our lives and we all need to be that someone to someone else. A prayer partner! There isn't a greater way to display our love for another woman in our lives. Jesus said it this way, "Greater love hath no man than this that a man lay down his life for his friends." (John 15:13 KJV)

Don't give up on the desires God has placed in your heart, whether it is finding that helpful friend, having children, deciding on a career path, finding peace with who you are, or being the trailblazer in your family by finishing high school. Continue to be brave by stepping out when doors of opportunity open up. One of the most empowering tools we have as women is our resilience, which exemplifies our inner strength, peace and beauty.

My deepest belief is that if you love God and come to Him empty, with no agenda (Isaiah 55:1), you will find that inner peace that will lead to your inner beauty. Inner peace...what a gift. This is where we will soar to the highest heights and have our greatest impact. This is where we will discover the buried God-given gifts and talents we have. When we become "quiet" within we appreciate more of who we are instead of comparing ourselves to another or rating our success on a distorted measure of what someone else's life looks like. When we have inner peace, we do what is right for the right reasons and with the most honourable motives. We may feel like we are losing if our path seems onerous and someone else's seems quick and easy. However, have we considered that our troublesome, burdensome path may be building our character for something beyond what we dare imagine? God says it this way in Ephesians 3:20, "Now to him who is able to do immeasurably more than all we ask or imagine, according to his power that is at work within us."

Have we considered that God sees the bigger picture and He is sometimes taking us along the path that will allow us to succeed in bigger and better ways? Have we considered that we are not ready for what we hoped to have yesterday? The Bible says the Lord is replenishing us with new wine. He is forcing us to grow so that we can stand in honour and strength in the new places He has prepared for us to venture into so that we can meet the people He has planned to cross our paths. If we cannot stretch, like a new wineskin, we will miss out on these opportunities and cause more strife. Therefore, we must trust that God is preparing us and He will cause us to triumph in the new spaces He has planned for us. (Matthew 9:16-17 NIV)

With God, our creator, we are valuable, and He makes none of our encounters wasteful. Our misfortunes are part of His plan too. God knows what He is doing with us. He will take care of us and will not abandon us. He plans to give us the future we hope for (Jeremiah 29:11 MSG). I dare you to keep believing and not cast away your hope!

ABOUT THE AUTHOR

S.S. Rich is an impassioned woman of God, a committed educator, and an avid proponent of well-being. As an educator, S.S. Rich is passionate about fostering healthy social and emotional development in her students. She regards a student's well-being as an essential foundation for their future success.

S.S. Rich also nurtures well-being in her own life through ongoing prayer, self-reflection, daily exercise, eating healthy, and getting enough rest. She attributes her inner strength and resolve to a deeply-rooted relationship with her faith, believes herself to be extravagantly rich, and that her personal growth and success is due to God's presence in her life.

CHAPTER 10

Being Authentic and Strong

by Maheeza Mohamed

I have always enjoyed interviews. Although they are a nerve-wracking experience, they contributed to some of the most memorable moments I've had in my career. Recently, I was interviewed by two friendly-looking gentlemen, John, a South American with short curly hair, heavy-set glasses, and William, a tall and slim Asian gentleman with a warm and friendly smile, sitting behind an executive table in a compact and sophisticated office room.

After the initial "tell us about yourself" introductory questions, John casually asked, "Tell me one thing people think of you and that they are totally wrong about?"

This took me by surprise, seeing that none of the many module interview question websites I studied vigorously suggested to prepare for such a question! Knowing that I had to come up with a unique response without putting my foot in my mouth, I was reminded of a time where one of my interview coaches, Samantha told me, "Be your authentic self and show your sense of humour."

Looking up at the interviewers, I smiled, nodded, and then, with a straight face said, "Because I wear the Hijab, most people assume I would be very laid back and soft-spoken…" As I was saying this, I could sense the tension between John and William as they may have been concerned about it becoming awkward. I continued without changing my serious expression, "…and then I'd open my mouth, giving them a culture shock." I joined them as they both burst out laughing.

As Albert Einstein said, "Once we accept our limits, we go beyond them." I have learned to accept that I will not always get an opportunity to let people know me before they categorize me into a societal stereotype; to accept that this unconscious bias exists although it shouldn't. When faced with such situations, I use my sense of humour to overcome awkwardness rather than get defensive.

A few years ago, I was just starting a new job and was in a training class with 14 others. It was a diverse group; everyone was very friendly, and we got along well. The trainer told each of us to speak a bit about where we were from if we were not born in Canada, for the ice breaker activity. We were placed at tables, set in two rows horizontal to each other, with a few at the end forming a U-shape. When it was my turn, as soon as I said that I was from Sri Lanka, Robert, a heavily built Jamaican gentleman started protesting that it simply could not be true. The class went into pin-drop silence and I broke the silence by laughing and asking him, "Okay, so you know better than me where I am from?"

Robert quickly explained, "All the Sri Lankans I have met have very dark skin, darker than mine, and I am Jamaican."

"Interesting! How many Sri Lankans have you met?" I asked playfully.

He rolled his eyes, started counting with his fingers, and said, "About five." The class started laughing at this point and I replied, "That's definitely a big percentage of our population!"

Then Philip, who had emigrated recently to Canada from the United States, asked, "So, are there a lot of Muslims in Sri Lanka?"

I replied, "Yes, there are, but we are a minority at around 11% of the population."

He took a quick look at my red scarf, grey cardigan, and multicoloured maxi dress, and said, "But I don't understand why most of your ladies in the Middle East wear black in that heat and men wear white and stay comfortable."

Again, I felt the same tension I felt in the interview room, in the classroom. Before I knew it, I replied, "Well, Philip, imagine if you saw me at a distance wearing white from head to toe in a dark alley. Wouldn't you think I was Casper the Friendly Ghost and be mortally frightened?" Philip and everyone else laughed, but I am sure they understood the irony in my responses.

Even though I joke around, I would be lying if I said I don't worry about the safety of my daughters who are 17 and 15, who also wear the Hijab; that I don't get anxiety when I see reports about hate crimes against ladies in Hijab on the news, or that I didn't get angry and upset when one of my former bosses harassed me for my faith, insinuating that I was a terrorist. It is very draining and frustrating at times to constantly need to overcome judgment, discrimination, and prejudice. I overcame them with the help of a few wonderful people of diverse faith and ethnicity that stood by me and stood up for me.

I must admit that sometimes the perceptions and stereotypes give me an advantage. You may wonder what the hell I am talking about. When I was about 15 years old, I went to an all Muslim girls' school in Colombo, the capital city of Sri Lanka. Especially in Colombo and other major cities, there was prestige attached to attending certain schools that produced great results in education, sports, and extracurricular activities like speech, dance, and drama. Our school was not necessarily one of them. The other schools didn't see us as equals when it came to inter-school competitions for debates, speech, and drama. In the 90s, it is safe to say that not much was done by our school or students to change that, but I wanted to do what I could to change it.

I captained a debate team for an inter-school debating contest, and we were up against the prestigious Catholic school named Trinity Convent. They didn't consider us a worthy opponent, giving us a big advantage. We put a lot of time and effort into preparation and won the contest. Preceding that, I was called to the teachers' staff room by my English teacher, Shazia. She said, "Maheeza, there is an impromptu English speech contest held by the Education Ministry. You would not stand a chance." I thought she was referring to my inexperience, but she went on to say, "against all the big schools." When trying to protest my opinion, my teacher quickly added, ignoring me, "...we do not expect you to win but to participate so that the Ministry doesn't think that our Muslim girls are always backward and do not show up." She was happy to add the icing on the cake as I was about to leave, "I heard the judge was racist against Muslims, so don't have any hopes of winning and get disappointed."

I wasn't sure whether my fist clenched in anger about my teacher's counter-productive pep talk or if I shook my head in disbelief that she expected me to accept discrimination as a norm.

I went to the contest at a neighbouring school and was directed to a classroom for my age group. There were many small groups of young girls and boys from different schools chatting and waiting for the contest to start. As I entered the classroom, I could feel all eyes on me with the all too familiar tension. No one spoke to me or acknowledged me, so I sat by myself in a corner and started reading quotes that I had collected in an old diary. At that time, I understood what my Uncle Pamo would constantly declare, "I would rather someone be rude to me than be indifferent." To me, there is no greater disrespect and insult than indifference.

When the judges announced that myself and a guy from a prestigious Kings College both won first place, the kids could not contain their astonishment. I felt a wicked sense of satisfaction to watch their jaws drop in dismay. To the surprise of my school and many others, I proceeded to win second in provincial and third in national level competitions.

As hard as it was to face Islamophobia and rejection from non-Muslims, I found it more painful when people of my faith gave me a hard time by imposing their personal opinions and prejudices as religion. There were two main ethnic minority groups of Muslims in Sri Lanka. Moors-Arab traders who settled in Sri Lanka, and Malays who were of Malaysian and Indonesian origin. My father was a Moor and my mother was a Malay. My mum, unfortunately, passed away when I was five and my dad remarried a Moor lady. She tended to discriminate towards my mother's race. When I was about 22, my stepmother asked whether I would marry a Moor or a Malay, to which I responded, "I would marry a Muslim."

My immediate family and our social circle consisted of conventional people. They would practice the main duties such as faith is monotheism, praying five times a day, fasting during the month of Ramadan, giving charity, and going on pilgrimage (if financially able). Ladies would wear modest traditional clothes like Saree and Salwar but were not covering their heads with a Hijab. If anyone challenged the norm then it was met with a lot of hostility and ridicule.

By now, you may have guessed that I had to challenge the norm. I studied our religion, taking extra classes in school, and embraced its principles on my own. I had quite the battle with my stepmom and her family when I chose to wear a Hijab at the age of 14. Yes, counter to the assumptions made by many, a Hijab was not forced upon me. I chose it myself.

I went through constant ridicule, judgmental stares, speeches of caution about how I would not be able to find a job or a suitor to marry me, all because I wore the Hijab. The famous words from my step-aunt Jamila would sum up the sentiments of many, *"This girl has been brainwashed by some extremist; she won't be able to find a job in this country. She will end up an old spinster, alone, as our guys like their wives to be modern."*

Today, I am proud to share with you that I married the love of my life and have three beautiful kids. A 17-year-old daughter and 15-year-old twins – son and daughter. I have worked in many multinational companies in different capacities in Sri Lanka and then I immigrated to Canada about 11 years ago.

When I immigrated, I was warned by many well-meaning friends and family that I wouldn't find a job in the Western world because I was in Hijab. Not only did I get jobs, but I advanced through them into leadership roles. I held many executive positions and delivered many speeches and workshops on leadership and public speaking, in Toastmasters, a nonprofit educational organization that operates clubs worldwide to promote communication, public speaking, and leadership. I am a proud Distinguished Toastmaster which is the highest educational award in the organization. It would not have been possible if I had let the negative ones decide what I can and cannot do.

My heart fills with pride when my two beautiful daughters, in Hijab, embrace their religion and faith without being deterred by Islamophobia. They, too, use humour to meet some of the mockeries about how we can hide our big hips and love handles under loose garments; how we will never have a bad hair day.

I encourage them to be authentic – to be resilient when faced with rejection and prejudice – and to learn and practice their faith for what it is, while respecting other religions and ethnicities and whatever other people choose to practise without imposing any of our beliefs or choices on anyone else, so that they, too, can reach their potential with positive, accepting, wonderful people in the world.

ABOUT THE AUTHOR

 Maheeza Mohamed has worked in the Telecommunications Industry for more than 20 years and currently works as a team manager in a major telecommunication company in Toronto, Canada. She survived a civil war for over 30 years, in Sri Lanka where she was born, before immigrating to Canada with her husband and three children in 2009. She lives in the Greater Toronto Area for a peaceful and safer life.

An artist, poet, and public speaker who is passionate about inclusion, diversity, and supporting people as they overcome challenges – through her own life experiences – Maheeza has delivered over 50 speeches and leadership workshops as a Distinguished Toastmaster. She loves expressing life through the arts of speech, painting, and writing. She is now looking forward to her newfound passion in Real Estate.

CHAPTER 11

Keeping My Vineyard and Sporting New Tires

by Angella Nunes

As I sit here looking at my painting, many thoughts and memories flood my mind. This painting, of a few tender green leaves of a sapling breaking through brown soil on a cloudy day, has tell-tale signs of amateur work. However, I can proudly say this is my work. It has a prominent place in my home but even more, this visual representation of my intention for 2020 has a cherished place in my heart.

I remember the morning of Saturday, January 11, 2020. The temperature was -10 degrees Celsius. The combination of rain, sleet, and snow was like large puffs of frozen cotton. For most of Southern Ontario, a travel advisory was in effect, but I was too excited about the day's event to cancel. I was going to a special New Year's event

— the theme was "Sip, Paint & GROW!" With this year being the start of a new decade and a 'Double 20' there was a lot of buzz and hype around having 20/20 vision. The organizer, Daisy Wright, proposed that this workshop would be the re-introduction of her 'Let's GROW' project. It was her 20/20 vision to bring together a generous and motivated group of women, committed to building give and take relationships to advance their careers and of others.

The representation in the meeting room had the resemblance of a United Nations women's caucus. In mocktail fashion, with non-alcoholic bubbly drinks in plastic flute glasses, we worked the room. The instruction given was that it was now January 2021. To celebrate, we would talk about what we had accomplished in the year 2020. The effect was whimsical! I shared my success which entailed roundtable talks with seasoned women who wanted to help our younger peers to GROW. I spoke of the impact of the honest, empowering conversations about weathering the storms of life situations while pursuing personal and professional development and climbing career ladders. The credibility was amazing! For the next activity, a young black female artist painstakingly guided us through the process of duplicating on canvas, a watercolour picture that would be symbolic of growth. I left that day with my 'GROW' painting on canvas and big plans in mind for a roundtable event in early spring 2020.

Sadly, COVID-19 arrived in Canada. This unwelcome guest with a smirk on its face was making its rounds globally. In March, our country succumbed to the pressure to lock down and the coronavirus watched maliciously while my plan rolled into oblivion like apples rolling downhill from a capsized applecart. What was I supposed to do? I had opted for early retirement and was thoroughly enjoying life. I had spent most of my working life inspiring breakthroughs for individuals who were struggling with making career decisions. That was my passion and I continued doing that – sometimes paid, but mostly pro-bono. Included in my 20/20 vision was the plan to become more intentional about entrepreneurship.

I decided to take advantage of virtual summits and online events, and there were many. I have always been vivacious, spontaneous, and curious so I welcomed these activities along with whatever career coaching opportunities that came my way. I went into overdrive, sometimes double-booking virtual events and taking in multiple seminars daily. Staying busy would keep the COVID-19 blues under control, I thought.

An amazing opportunity for group coaching came my way. I was invited to join a group of women for an informal Bible study. At the time, there were five women and I would be number six. These ladies were a fun bunch. It was a wonderful social connection, so I committed to it. After all, since we had to be on lockdown anyway, why not? A few days in, I was nominated as the "teacher" of the group. This was unexpected and I felt somewhat unprepared, but I welcomed the challenge.

In a roundabout way, we settled on the book, Song of Solomon, written by King Solomon. This English translation of a romantic song, originally written in old Hebrew, was eight brief chapters. Often appearing on screen, the storyline holds some very descriptive scenes of steamy, suggestive, sensual encounters between the king and a peasant farm girl; hardly the kind of story one would expect to find in the Bible. The book was an engaging read of provocative content. A good mix of misfortune and ecstasy with terms of endearment that today might sound like insults, our reading resulted in tear-jerkers amid bouts of hysterical laughter. Juicy and spicy!

The word about this group spread among friends like wildfire. Within a week, we were up to 16 women joining us every day, Monday to Friday from 11:00 a.m. to 1:30 p.m. We also had interest from others who could only connect occasionally but still wanted to be a part of this juicy, spicy tribe.

There was mention of the lovers lying in the meadow and sensory expressions of the gardens and the pomegranate orchard but there was much more to this little book than only a love song. I imagined inhaling the delightful scents from trees, flowers, and herbs. I was curious to know more about the spices and essential oils made from the trees and herbs that could be compounded to be used as fragrances and ointments.

The women connected well. Together, we spoke of the joy of hanging clusters of camphire flowers as an air freshener as well as the benefits to hair and skin from dye made from the camphire leaves, known as henna. We discussed the effective home remedies made from the delicate saffron flower that were passed down through generations as well as our own concoctions that cure all kinds of ailments – from skin conditions to improving libido. When we got to talking about the many uses for cinnamon, my taste buds were tantalized to the point of drooling. Snickerdoodle cookies, the many ways to use cinnamon to spice up your porridge, teas, and beverages; I wanted to try them all.

A pivotal moment came as we exegeted the words:

> *"...They made me a keeper of the vineyards, but my own vineyard have I not kept..." (Song of Solomon 1:6)*

We started to notice life lessons and out came my life coach hat. The women were open to having a deeper experience and the group became a safe space that allowed for transparency and vulnerability. We engaged in activities and exercises that would maximize and reinforce this learning experience. It was quite okay to lament over regrets, missed opportunities, and unfulfilled dreams. There was space to write affirmations, list aspirations, and share them. Each person even committed to creating a vision board called, "My Vineyard!"

After a couple of weeks, we decided to take Wednesdays off. It was exhausting for me to prepare the lessons each day, but it was gratifying to hear impact statements about the growth that was occurring within the group. These women spoke with exuberance about the transformation that they were experiencing, and I was truly overjoyed. Yet there was a little voice on the inside asking, "What about you?" This was my moment of truth. The desire for career coaching had begun to feel like a glass of cola left out overnight. It was still sweet but the fizz was gone. An offer for partnership presented itself and I agreed to consider it, but I felt a gnawing discontent on the inside. Great idea, and flattering though it was, my heart was not in it. No spark, no fizz.

I realized that I desperately needed to interrupt my pattern. For years, my method of operation had always been to establish protocol, maintain confidentiality, navigate obstacles, motivate, encourage, and support others, regardless of my personal needs. It didn't matter about me if the process was successful. But now, there was a dilemma – the rescuer in me needed to be rescued. While everyone was experiencing breakthroughs, I was busy safeguarding my issues. I kept them under lock and key in the innermost chambers of my heart. The isolation and seclusion had made me as much a victim of the effects of this pandemic as everyone else. Being housebound was taking its toll. Additionally, one of my daughters was hundreds of miles away dealing with a major life crisis. The ache of that reality was constantly playing monopoly in my head and my heart while I sought ways to keep moving this group forward.

"My own vineyard have I not kept…"

While they were gaining clarity on aspirations, was it time for me to redefine my purpose and bucket list?

I began to realize that I was a part of this group for a reason — these people had become my friends and I needed them as much as they needed me. They trusted me with their struggles, and we were in this together. I had been invited as a participant, not as the group facilitator. This role emerged and I was good at it but now, "Physician, heal thyself!"

I often choose to suffer in silence, laugh, and appear to hold it together, but with the pandemic, this was like carrying a ton of bricks. This was an unprecedented season. A new normal was required to handle the stress and challenges that came with it. I wondered if the thumping of my heart was audible. Not good. I had gone through a cardiac event a few years prior so if this is a warning, then I must take heed.

Time to make that decision. Okay, okay. Deep breaths…here we go.

The day that I took the risk and bared my soul, these women were ready for it. I felt as if I stumbled into a doorway and had fallen through helplessly. Little did I know that they had been waiting for me with their arms open wide. The nurturing vibes in their voices held me ever so gently. They had ready words and prayers, like fragrant ointment, for all that ailed me. The dam behind my eyeballs broke and tears flowed uncontrollably down my cheeks. They cried too. I could feel the tension leaving my shoulders as I accepted the same spiritual and emotional support that the others had received around this very intimate friendship table.

What a relief! Take deep breaths, nice and slow. Say no more. I came to realize that this was indeed the table that I had envisioned at the Sip, Paint & GROW event. I had a huge sense of gratitude to be able to experience it firsthand.

We decided to share facilitation within the group which required a little coaxing for some, but the opportunity allowed them to see how much they had grown. I found easing into this format to be very invigorating for me as well. Sometimes to GROW, some elements may have to be pruned so that others may develop. I now willingly accept the nurturing environment created by trusted friends both within this circle and beyond when my soul gets weary.

A few weeks ago, I planted six lima beans in a mason jar with water and paper towel. As they grew, the jar crowded with sprouts reminded me of the way my mind had become with all that I had been taking in and carrying all by myself. I am happy to say that my bean plants are now thriving in an environment that was required. Clearing my head and my heart has also made room for new sprouts and new branches and I feel great. With this transformation, I can now welcome the new opportunities that are coming my way. Ah, yes! There's nothing like pouring a glass of cola that has so much fizz that it tickles your nose.

Someone recently offered me a new definition for the word "re-tire." "It means putting on new tires. Get it?" she asked. "Re-Tire?" I chuckled at first but as I give it more thought, this definition seems about right. For me, GROWing means that I am *keeping my own vineyard and sporting new tires.*

ABOUT THE AUTHOR

 Angella Nunes is a recently retired Adult Educator and Career Development Practitioner who worked in the Ontario College system for 27 years, educating, empowering, and inspiring career development. She is also actively involved as a church and community volunteer. Angella finds fulfilment in helping others overcome the obstacles that are keeping them from getting ahead, supporting them in their struggles, and celebrating their breakthroughs.

Throughout Angella's career, she has had the pleasure of serving on the executive of several professional associations and advisory boards but the experience of being a wife, a mother of four wonderful human beings, and a grandmother of five precious jewels, is her greatest joy.

linkedin.com/in/angellanunes

CHAPTER 12

Lessons Learned While Navigating the Workplace

by Alicia Sullivan

"What I know for sure is that speaking your truth is the most powerful tool we all have." – Oprah Winfrey

Graduating from university with a master's degree and landing a job as a senior policy analyst was like winning the jackpot for a young woman from humble beginnings. I was ready for a progressive and fulfilling career. Then we immigrated to Canada from my beautiful homeland, Jamaica. I arrived in Canada over a decade and a half ago with my partner and our toddler. As the airplane landed on the tarmac at Pearson International Airport in Toronto one cold fall night, I sensed that our lives would change forever.

I chose Canada as my new home because I wanted to make the most of its opportunities for myself and my family. However, the truth is, I was scared that I didn't know how to do this in an unfamiliar place where there were so few people of colour in my circle who were in positions of influence. Self-doubt crept in after initial limited success in finding career-related positions. My first job was working as a sales associate in a retail clothing store where I folded clothes, Swiffered change rooms, restocked shelves, and enthusiastically greeted customers with the latest promotion. My colleagues were primarily high school girls and there I was, a grown woman of professional standing, folding clothes to earn a living. As you may have guessed, I felt unfulfilled and my faith and self-esteem waned. Although I felt discouraged, when I looked at my little girl each day, I remembered why I came to Canada – to pursue a better life for her and our future generations. I knew that I had to keep seeking opportunities that were more in line with my goals.

One day I was reading a local newspaper when an article sparked my interest in an organization that was pursuing social research. Given my prior experience and career goals, I felt inspired to reach out to express an interest in volunteering. Before long, I was juggling a retail job, a call centre role, and volunteering on this research project. When a paid position opened up, I applied and was successful. This was a turning point for me but in the early years, I struggled to adjust to Canadian workplace culture. After four years, I resigned from this position to pursue further studies while raising a family.

In retrospect, leaving this job before gaining a firm foundation in the Canadian workplace and without a professional network, was one of the biggest career mistakes I've made. The next few years were particularly difficult as I regressed both personally and professionally. My self-image took a nosedive and I experienced the darkest and most heartrending period of my life. Everything fell apart in the fourth year after I left this job – my outlook on life, health, marriage, and finances. The 'better' life that I envisioned was now way off-course and I was forced to make some tough decisions.

In hindsight, this was a time for transformation. First, I hit rock bottom and was confronted with challenges in every aspect of my life. For a long time, I had played it safe and lacked the will and confidence to take full responsibility and now the rug was pulled out from under me. It was through serendipity that I was introduced to personal development resources which I consumed day and night. I then discovered that for things to change I had to change, and for things to get better, I had to become better (Jim Rohn). This process opened my eyes to the truth that my life was exactly a reflection of my mindset and the decisions I made each step of the way. I was forced to take personal responsibility for everything – the good, the bad and the indifferent. This was a hard pill to swallow and led to many sleepless nights and soaked pillows, but because I stuck with the process, I overcame the challenges. Some of the daily practices which I've adopted include visualization, gratitude journalling, practising affirmations, reading and listening to self-help resources, and applying suggested practices. I also intentionally surrounded myself with positive associations. These practices continue to serve me well to this day.

After a few years, I was privileged to return to my previous employer to pursue a role as a Senior Associate that felt meaningful to me. I was now more self-aware, confident, and purposeful, and was determined to contribute more significantly this time around. I pushed myself beyond my comfort zone while enjoying the work and staying motivated, resulting in a quick promotion to Director. Thanks to the intentional advocacy of an executive who sponsored me, I was afforded high impact stretch opportunities (e.g. working directly with corporations and firms on their diversity and inclusion strategy and programming, presenting at conferences, leading workshops designed for leaders, etc.) which I otherwise would not have been considered for. These opportunities helped me to hone my strengths while improving on gaps in my skills. My sponsor modelled characteristics of an inclusive leader – humility, authenticity, empathy – and took a personal interest in my success. I'm forever grateful to have had the opportunity to work with this leader.

One of the opportunities for me to contribute beyond my usual role presented itself when I was tapped to be the master of ceremonies for the organization's annual conference in Canada. I had never done this in a professional capacity before, but I always say yes when I'm called upon to do something and then figure out how to do it later. On the morning of the diversity and inclusion conference, while in transit, I pictured myself being authentic, confident, and engaging. The program went over well and I was glad that I said yes to this new experience.

Hosting the Canadian event led to the pivotal opportunity of co-hosting the organization's global conference in New York City a few months later. About a week before the big event, one of the event organizers reached out to ask whether I wanted to be a master of ceremonies for the signature conference which attracted over 800 business leaders from across the world. I said yes with no hesitation. This was an incredible opportunity to continue contributing beyond my day-to-day role. On the day of the event, as soon as I awoke in a midtown NYC hotel room, I picked up my deck of affirmation cards and the first statement to surface read,

> *"It's not what a job brings me that matters but what I bring to a job. No job is above me nor beneath me. The job is important because it is in front of me." (author unknown)*

This was a prescient message which reminded me that the task ahead – co-hosting the conference – was 'in front of me' to be accomplished with poise and excellence.

I knew in my heart that it would be a phenomenal day. As the time for the event kickoff approached, I felt unstoppable and was ready to bring my 'A' game. I pinched myself knowing that I would have a once-in-a-lifetime privilege of meeting and sharing the stage with some outstanding corporate leaders. This is a day I will never forget. The experience provided an indelible boost to my confidence which catapulted me into many opportunities, several of which challenged me to develop more advanced skills and competencies. I employed diligence and grit and prepared well to execute each assignment to the best of my ability.

I'm cognizant that the time I spent with this employer offered me huge professional development. I continue to pursue work that is meaningful to me as a human rights, diversity, equity, and inclusion professional. I intend to make a lasting mark doing what I've been called to do – levelling the playing field for everyone in the spaces I'm privileged to occupy.

As I reflect, however, I'm reminded that during this time of professional progress, crucial areas of my personal life were challenged. For example, I was going through a family legal process and I had athletic children participating in competitive activities which demanded much of my time and energy. Juggling work and my personal life required tremendous effort. I was burnt out from burning the candle at both ends, investing a lot of time outside of work hours to deliver strong results while caring for my children almost single-handedly and shuttling them to and from activities, six days per week.

Over time, this took a toll on my physical and emotional well-being. I remember driving in the express lanes on a busy freeway with my kids and experiencing two episodic panic attacks in the space of ten minutes. After the second incident, I was forced to exit the highway, parked the car, and stepped out to catch my breath. When the physical sensations subsided, I continued on my way home, all the while aware of the thought, *"What if this strange overwhelming, head-raising, dizzying, nauseating, sweat-inducing feeling returns while I'm driving?"* I was relieved to arrive home safely.

This was a wake-up call for me. I was overstressed and my body was signalling that this pace was unsustainable. At that moment, I decided to step back to re-channel my efforts towards self-care and my family. I have no regrets about this decision.

I share this story to remind us that life is always happening to and for us, simultaneously. While one aspect of my life (growing my career) made me feel accomplished, an imbalance with the demands of other areas negatively impacted my overall well-being. I had to take responsibility and choose what was more important to me at that moment.

Here are three lessons that I've learned as I've navigated the workplace:

1. Leap before you are ready

   Like many women, my natural inclination is to be one hundred per cent ready before I take on a new opportunity. I feel compelled to obtain the right credentials, wait for the perfect time, meet the right people, etc. What I've discovered is that there is no perfect timing or formula for charting one's career path. If you are going to have a fulfilling career, you must act in the face of uncertainty and without all the answers and skills. Once you have the aptitude and desire to learn and grow, additional skills can be developed with proper support over time. You will make mistakes, fail, and experience setbacks in the process, but the lessons learnt will be invaluable for the next opportunity. I suggest you keep failing forward on your career journey.

2. You are your best advocate – ask for the next stretch opportunity

   I wish I learnt this lesson early on when I transitioned into the Canadian workforce. You must ask for what you want – the next opportunity, the salary, and how you want to be treated. Many of the career breakthroughs that have opened for me happened when I revealed what I wanted to people in positions of influence. Tell your manager, sponsor, and professionals who you admire, what you want and ask them for advice to help you realize your goals and aspirations. This requires an incredible amount of preparation, perseverance, and vulnerability, but taking this risk can lead to a greater understanding of what it takes: alignment and advocacy to get you where you want to go.

3. If you are in a position of influence take a chance on people of colour
    People of colour lag behind their white colleagues when it comes to getting hired and promoted. For the most part, it is not a lack of drive or credentials that hold them back, but the systems within which they operate – structured, historically, to be advantageous to some people more than others. I've come to realize that some spaces were not necessarily designed with people of colour in mind and when we enter places where we were once unwelcome, or there are few of us, many of us struggle to thrive. Given this, I encourage anyone in a position to hire, promote, mentor or sponsor people of colour, to do so. Just give them a chance – show them the ropes and actively invest your social and professional capital to support their development. You'll be glad you did because from what I know, people of colour are dedicated, resilient, and have an innate desire to succeed when space is allowed for their authentic voice and unmasked presence.

Not long ago, a friend and I had a heart-to-heart chat. We reminisced about our core values, philosophies, and projected future aspirations. After the call, I received a text message which read, *"You have grown beautifully in every way…"* I smiled, graciously accepting this generous compliment and intentionally paused for self-appreciation. I reflected on the journey that had taken me this far and marvelled at the thought that I have come a long way, although I've still got much further to go.

ABOUT THE AUTHOR

Alicia Sullivan has answered the calling to be a force for equity and social justice. The recipient of a law degree and a master's degree, Alicia currently works in higher education promoting respect for everyone's human rights and dignity. Alicia is devoted to using her time and energy to influence organizational change, enabling a culture of inclusion where diverse people experience a sense of belonging and can fully contribute.

Before this role, Alicia worked in the nonprofit sector consulting with corporations and firms on their initiatives and programs to accelerate gender equality. She also worked internationally, overseeing a research program which monitored the socioeconomic conditions of a population.

Alicia volunteers with The Backpack Project, Girl. Strong, the Canadian Caribbean Association of Halton, and the Halton District School Board Equity and Inclusion Education Steering Advisory Committee. Her inspiration comes from her desire for a world where her children and future generations are treated equitably and can maximize their full potential.

linkedin.com/in/alicia-a-sullivan

CHAPTER 13

Challenges Build Resilience

by Melissa Enmore

The sun must have been piercing through those hospital windows on that scorching hot day when I decided to make my grand entrance into the world. I imagine my parents being as excited as they were scared, having just become parents for the very first time. I'm sure that although my parents were relieved to have a healthy, happy baby, they couldn't help but wonder – what kind of child I would be, what my personality would be like, whether I would be smart, what I would be when I grew up, and whether I would make them proud.

When I reflect on my childhood, I smile because it was a happy one. I grew up in a two-parent home in Georgetown, Guyana. My dad worked and my mom was a homemaker who took exceptional care of my younger brother and me. Although I was a little "chatterbox" as my mom would say, who asked a million questions, she never once complained about my curiosity or about me sharing every detail of every day. But she never missed an opportunity to remind me, in good ole Guyanese fashion, "girl your ears hard," meaning I was stubborn. In my defence, I am a Taurus.

I loved that my mom was always there for me, to listen, answer my questions, read with and to me, and have conversations anytime I wanted, although I usually did most of the talking. She instilled a level of confidence in me that would prove beneficial throughout my teenage years and well into adulthood. The spiritual leader in our home, my mom was a gentle giant who was militant about prayer, bible studies, and our relationship with God, always reminding us to put God first. My mom was such a great mom, that I often wonder if I could ever fill her shoes.

When my dad returned from his business travels, after distributing the sweet treats he brought home for us, he would share stories about his island adventures and long nights spent working on reports. I admired his work ethic, and how much he was respected and admired by his colleagues. He instilled in me the importance of education and the value of hard work. As a result, I was a good student but evidently, never good enough when it came to the high standards my dad set. Nonetheless, I kept pushing and striving – I wanted to do better.

If I came home with a 98% – which would probably make most parents happy – my dad would ask me about the 2%. That's how much he pushed me to be not just good or great, but exceptional. God forbid he caught me slacking off or watching too much television! He would gently remind me that my high-performing classmates were probably studying. He taught me how to play chess, which is when I realized just how fiercely competitive I was, and a very sore loser too, breaking down and sobbing when I lost. It wasn't over until I won and I was always determined to win. The fighter in me could not accept defeat.

I can only recall having one serious illness – pneumonia – but I was told that as a child, I was sick and hospitalized a few times, giving my parents quite the scare. However, I am quite sure that the fighter in me was developed during these times and helped to mould me into the woman I am today, a resilient woman. Not to mention the fact that I grew up with a brother and male cousins; I had to be tough to survive.

When my dad came home and shared the news, "We are moving to Canada," I was intrigued and became curious about this new adventure. Moving meant that I wouldn't see my friends and cousins for an awfully long time (if ever again) and as a teenager, my friends and cousins were the equivalents of Wi-Fi. However, moving also meant that I would be able to see another part of the world I had never travelled to – North America.

I can still remember unbuckling my seatbelt a few times to adjust my Walkman on our red-eye flight to Canada. My best friends and cousins had accompanied us to the airport that night to see us off. As sad as I was, I eagerly anticipated what was in store for me. All I knew about Canada was that it was extremely cold. My teenage mind could not even fathom what my parents were thinking or feeling about this enormous life change. But they continually reassured us that we were moving so that my brother and I could have a better life and more opportunities. There was no turning back.

When we finally arrived on Canadian soil, it was not what I expected. For starters, I became extremely self-conscious and astutely aware of my dark skin, broad nose, kinky hair, and curvy body. The culture shock was real and left me feeling out of place, despite having family friends to assist with the transition.

As if being a teenager wasn't hard enough, I had to adapt to a new country, new school, new seasons and of course, a new culture. It was a lot and I often erupted in emotional outbursts about why my parents would leave the beautiful Caribbean breeze to come here to freeze. Meanwhile, my eight-year-old brother was busy making new friends, snowmen, and sports teams. I was so jealous of how easy it was for him to adjust, but I became determined to adapt as well.

As a student in Guyana's British education system where high school started at age 11 and 10 subjects were taught each semester, I was able to thrive. This allowed for a seamless academic transition to the Canadian high school system. While good grades didn't require much effort on my part, I became very complacent with my studies. The wake-up call came in my first year of undergraduate studies at the University of Toronto when I almost failed my first year. This was my first real encounter with failure and I hated it. I quickly smartened up, adjusted my study habits, and got back on track academically.

My first real failure taught me a lot about myself. I was mortified but determined to course-correct because I couldn't disappoint my parents – they'd worked too hard to give me this opportunity. But also, I felt like I needed to do well for my community. In my short time in Canada, I couldn't help but notice that as I advanced in my academic and professional career, there were fewer and fewer people who look like me. This bothered me a lot but made me even more determined to do well and to show them what I was made of; educators, employers, and everyone else with doubts about my capabilities.

After university, I reconnected with a Guyanese classmate, Anna, who had since migrated to Trinidad. We soon realized that we both shared a deep love for children and for giving back to our community. In 2008, we came together (virtually) and co-founded The Backpack Project International Program, a nonprofit organization created to assist Caribbean children with their health and education. After a successful pilot launch in 2009, each year we provided pre-packed backpacks filled with stationery items (notebooks, pens, etc.) and personal health items (toothbrushes, toothpaste, etc.) to students in need. We were determined to make a difference in the world and there was no turning back.

After the catastrophic magnitude 7 earthquake in Haiti in 2010, we distributed backpacks to Haitian students. After the devastating category 5 Hurricane Irma ravaged several Caribbean islands in 2017, we provided backpacks to hurricane victims in St. Maarten. During COVID-19 in 2020, we partnered with Helping Hands Jamaica Foundation to distribute backpacks to students in Jamaica. Not only has The Backpack Project expanded to other islands over the years, but we have expanded in Toronto, Canada, through partnerships with various community organizations and school boards. Today, I remain as passionate about helping children as the day I started, and I am determined to use my skills, talents and abilities, to continue to serve students in need and make an impact in children's lives, one backpack at a time.

Leading The Backpack Project allows me the privilege of being sur-rounded by a team of beautiful, intelligent, classy, confident black women. Genuine friendship is so refreshing in a culture where it often seems that people are only friendly because of what they can gain from the "friendship." Like my dad, these women set the bar pretty high and expect nothing less of me. Over the years, they've pushed me to be better and aim higher, and the bonus is that we have now formed an incredible sisterhood. This proved to be par-ticularly beneficial during one of the most difficult periods in our history – dealing with the 2020 global pandemic. We were and continue to be a support system for each other. This was a big deal for me as I often struggle with female friendships.

As a little girl, I faced the harsh reality that jealousy is often in-tertwined in female friendships. At age 10, I distinctly remember the chaos that resulted from a missing notebook with my com-pleted homework. The situation quickly escalated to the point where my close friend's parents got involved, and eventually, the notebook magically appeared after its strategic placement at the back of my friend's closet. I remember being so confused about this incident that my parents had to explain it to me, "She was jealous that you did well in school." I remember thinking, "Why would you do that to a friend?" I had several other similar en-counters throughout my high school and university years, and even in the workplace – female jealousy. This is where I echo feminist Chimamanda Ngozi Adichie's line in Beyonce's song, Flawless, where she noted, "We raise girls to see each other as competitors. Not for jobs or for accomplishments, which I think can be a good thing, but for the attention of men."

Fighting for men's attention was always one of the least of my con-cerns. I happen to get more than enough attention from the amazing man I am dating, who is as intelligent as he is handsome. Although there was a time when I was sceptical about the idea of marriage and having family of my own – being cognizant of the divorce rate and our society's approach to family – I am now determined to have a family, define what my family will look like, and be intentional about integrating both traditional and modern elements in my family. I'm so thankful that I was stubborn enough to resist the pressure from family and friends to get married at a younger age or I would have been divorced, maybe twice by now. I'm glad I allowed myself time to grow into the woman that I am today.

An optimist by nature, I am typically a happy camper, full of life and energy. However, when COVID-19 was declared a global pandemic, I remember sitting on my couch and desperately trying to make sense of it all. That's when, in my moment of quiet reflection, it hit me – the importance of my journey to date and the lessons learned along the way.

My mom encouraged me to be curious and insisted that I stay close to God. My dad encouraged me to work and study hard, aim high, and never settle. Moving to Canada taught me to adapt to change, and failure taught me the importance of preparation. Sickness helped to develop the fighter in me and the resilience needed to get through these tough times. Helping others has brought so much fulfilment into my life, and as Tony Robbins often says, "Success without fulfillment is the ultimate failure." As I sit back and reflect, I realize that everything in my past was preparing me for this present moment. I remain hopeful that with my dogged determination, I will get through this pandemic, find opportunity amidst the chaos, and thrive on the other side. I believe that God has great work for me to do and He will continue to lead and equip me to do it.

ABOUT THE AUTHOR

A Guyanese native, Melissa Enmore is a passionate, energetic, and dynamic leader, speaker, connector, and change agent, with over 13 years of public and private sector Canadian healthcare experience. She is known for her ability to drive organizational change and deliver quality results. Her expertise is in the enablement of digital transformation, having led several strategic health initiatives that promote system integration and connectedness.

Melissa obtained a Bachelor of Science degree from the University of Toronto, and later a Master of International Public Health degree from the University of Queensland. She is also a certified project and change management professional.

Melissa is actively involved in her community. She is the Co-Founder and Director of The Backpack Project International Program, a nonprofit organization that assists Caribbean children and children of the Caribbean diaspora with their health and education. She is determined to make a difference in children's lives, one backpack at a time.

Melissa Enmore, MIPH, PMP, CMP (Prosci), CPHIMS-CA

LinkedIn:
https://www.linkedin.com/in/melissa-enmore-6052ab17/

YouTube Channel (Change with ME):
https://www.youtube.com/channel/
UCOzQHYLeVLkp1Aod2akiM8g/featured?view_as=subscriber

Facebook – The Backpack Project:
https://www.facebook.com/TheBackpackProject

Twitter – The Backpack Project:
https://twitter.com/bpp_caribbean

Instagram – The Backpack Project:
https://www.instagram.com/
the_backpack_project_caribbean

CHAPTER 14

Winggie Fly!

by Gloria Smith

Life's journey is like a highway, wide with many exits, laden with off-ramps, and sometimes we don't know where these exits will take us. Winggie would discover that at each off-ramp she stopped at, she would fly away a little stronger than from her previous destination. Her journey has not yet ended, and from the time she was nine years old, her ride along the highway of life has been breathtaking. Winggie has had many off-ramp experiences, one of which took place at Saint Michael Primary.

Winggie had big plans to take her common entrance exam to attend Wolmer's High School in Jamaica. In preparation, she took private lessons and stayed up late studying while burning a 'home sweet home' lamp. Daily, she would journey from West Kingston to East Kingston. Her day started at 7:00 a.m. when she took the JOS (Jamaica Omnibus Service), from Denham Town and made a stop in Parade Square to arrive at 6a Tower Street. Pushing her way on the bus, she hoped people would feel sorry for her and give her a seat because she had to arrive at school on time to avoid the wrath of Miss Bigsby's cane lashings. This teacher taught Winggie how to be punctual while beating the fear of God into her. Up until this day, she gets nervous if she is late.

Saint Michael Primary was located right beside the Tower Street Correctional Centre. Winggie fearfully passed tall walls with barbed wire and prisoners working outside on government programs daily. Prisoners escaped regularly and would run through the school which was a terrifying experience. While children played dandy shandy – a game which involved three children, two of whom threw a ball at a child standing in the middle of them, and once the ball hit the child in the middle, they lost their position to the child who hit them with the ball – or hopscotch during recess, escaped prisoners used them as human shields. Lockdowns at Saint Michael Primary had been a regular occurrence for many years. While attending Saint Michael, she experienced the fear of death, daily, on the playground. To this day, Saint Michael is struggling because of the violence in the surrounding community, as per The Gleaner newspaper headline dated July 20, 2020, "As Bullets Fly, Kids Cower behind Saint Michael's Shield." These petrifying experiences kept her in constant flight mode from danger.

Jamaicans are known for dressing with flair and elegance, and Saint Michael's school uniform was a testament to style. All students had to dress prim and proper, every day. Blue skirt pleats were stiffened using starch and were as stiff as soldiers guarding Buckingham Palace. White blouses washed with blue soap were very white, with no rings around the collars. Winggie hated the teacher's daily hygiene inspections. They would use a cane to slightly ease up skirts, smell students' breath, and inspect hair to make sure it was freshly combed. Winggie's fondest memory of Saint Michael School was singing the early morning hymns and prayers. Everyone had to know the Our Father prayer, the 23rd Psalm, the Beatitudes, Matthew 5, verses 1 to 12, and Proverbs 3, verses 1 to 6. During these sessions, she learned how to depend on God's love and mercy.

Winggie's best friends were Sandra, Sharon, and Judith. Judith lived at Foster Lane and the girls enjoyed playing in her backyard after school. Often, they bought hot bread and butter with their bus fares before they walked to her home. Sometimes, the four girls found themselves hanging around gang bangers out of fear and for physical protection. Flattop, Patricia, and Delroy were lawbreakers who befriended the girls. Patricia was dating Flattop. One day she was standing at the school gate in deep conversation with another fellow. Flattop, feeling disrespected by Patricia's action, threw a large stone at her head screaming, "Gal teck that!" Blood flowed from her head like Dunn's River Falls. Patricia went to the hospital to be treated. No one understood why, but by the next day, her relationship with Flattop was normal. This was one of Winggie's experiences of abuse and it taught her to never tolerate an abusive relationship. "Abusers do not let the door hit you on your way out." Now she runs from abusive people, whether they're male or female.

At the age of nine, Winggie's parents emigrated from Jamaica without her. She moved to her aunt's home which was located at 47 Lincoln Avenue in the Maxfield Avenue area. She felt afraid, lonely, abandoned, and unloved by the separation from her parents. Molested by a family member only to be told she was lying, Winggie became a statistic who had to adapt quickly to her new living arrangement. Imagine, a little girl of nine, weighing 75 pounds, with bird legs and brown hair struggling to survive without her parents! She adapted to her new environment but became mad as hell. Most adults at that time didn't realize they were doing more harm than good when they would beat children with the panganat whip (a whip from the pomegranate tree). Winggie learned to take the whippings and her weeping only lasted during the nights as peace came with daylight.

At the age of 12, on December 19, 1974, Winggie left Jamaica to go to the snow-white country of Canada. A kind and caring airline hostess looked after four children including Winggie on her first plane ride to Canada. Before landing, one of the children muttered, "I see this ya country rich. Dem even spread white sheet pon the ground." The snow on the ground looked like her grandmother's white sheets from the aerial view, but little did she know that Canada's white sheets were just cold snow.

Unlike in Jamaica where people dressed with elegance, Winggie's parents purchased a purple Eskimo coat with a hoodie and rubber boots with thick insoles to keep her warm. At that time, there were 32 centimetres of snow on the ground and the days were frigid cold. Winggie didn't care about her new winter gear or about being with her dad and family, she just wanted to go home! She had lost her friends and some family members because of the move.

Winggie's family lived in a box called an apartment, until they moved to Clarkson. In Jamaica, even if you lived in a one-room house, you still enjoyed the sunshine in the yard and freedom. Living in an apartment meant tenants could not laugh loudly, run in the house, or listen to loud music. Observing the snow falling through a window or watching the four-channel idiot box, also known as television, were normal pastimes. There was never a time she played outside.

School was another shock for Winggie. Being the only black child in her classes and not understanding Canadian culture led to very trying times. Students behaved in hurtful ways: name-calling, placing chewed gum in her afro, and leaving sharp pencils on her seat. On her first day of school, a young boy by the name of Dave greeted her while she was walking to school and changed her name from Winggie to Nigger. He made a big mistake that day. In the morning, she thought her new nickname was cute, but after returning home from lunch the dynamic changed. She ended up giving him a bloody nose and although she received detention, Dave never called her names again. Complaining to any school official was a waste of energy and there was a lack of support. Teachers would say, "Don't worry they are just having fun." Guidance counsellors discouraged her when she asked them about going to college, and one stated, "Don't worry about going to college or university. Canada has many factory jobs where you can work until you retire."

Winggie's experience with racism in her Canadian secondary school was unforgettable. Racism was prevalent back then and practised openly despite people exclaiming, "No, Canada? Never!" However, the actions of a few racists solidified the pain Winggie felt from leaving home – the land of wood and water, family, and loving friends. She used to be so angry when faced with racism, that she would pass out in the hallway of her high school. Eventually, Winggie adapted and coped with this new evil, and her determination not to live the life educators planned for her, pushed her to excel.

Looking back, Winggie believed that some white teachers and peers thought she would take their possessions and positions if she advanced herself with quality education. Blacks were teased so badly then, that sometimes, physical fights occurred. Blacks fought, marched, and suffered in silence with racism. No one listened, even if the authorities were notified about their struggles, incidents of systematic racism, bullying, and name-calling. For example, in high school, chocolate milk was thrown at the lunch table where Black children ate. Everything was always their fault but complaints fell on deaf ears. Back then, Blacks supported each other to combat racism, learning how to fight hard when no one was looking until eventually gaining respect.

Attending college to study accounting was the best choice Winggie made. She met some teachers who positively impacted her, and one teacher taught her how to avoid the social trap of welfare. After she left college, she worked for Bell Canada, where she met some awesome people. The first was Agnes, who taught her the power of shopping once a week and buying in bulk to save time and money. Agnes told her to buy big bags of rice, peas, cornmeal, and sugar. At that time, Winggie was a single mom of two children. Linda taught Winggie how to save by forcing her to invest 10 % worth of her earnings of Bell Canada stocks. One day she slammed a blue piece of paper on the lunch table and said, "Sign here! Young people do not know how to save. You are going to thank me later, even after I die!" Linda would check on Winggie mid-year to make sure she didn't cash in her stocks.

Winggie loved to shop till she dropped. A shopping junkie, she would buy 16 dresses in one afternoon as working at Bell Canada gave her the freedom to buy whatever she wanted for her family. Her co-workers, Wayne, and Perry were not impressed. One long weekend they refused to give her vacation time to shop in New York. Instead, they gave her a real estate book and asked, "Can you read?" "Yes?" she replied. "Yes!" her boss replied. "Winggie, there is no free ride in life. You either pay now or pay later... There is no free ride. You need to own a house," they commanded. Think about your children! Life lessons from these co-workers inspired Winggie to manage her finances and then later purchase her first home. Instead of her being homeless, she had a HOUSE full and sheltered many homeless people from Ghana, Tobago, Jamaica, and even Canada. And guess what? They were all white people. Surprised? At the time, Winggie was mad at them. How dare these white people tell her what to do! Funnily enough, she took their advice and the rest is history. She now reaps the benefits of their wise counsel.

Her experiences at the different off-ramps of life prepared Winggie for Covid-19. At every stage of her life, her challenges were different, but she survived. She survived the violent playground of Saint Michael School, she survived the abandonment by her parents when they emigrated from Jamaica, and she survived sexual abuse in Jamaica and racism during her formative years in Canada's school system. Winggie learned to adjust to every situation and adapt those lessons to her life. Her teachers in Jamaica taught her discipline and how to love God. Her experiences with racism helped her to fight for her rights and stand up against injustice. Her coworkers and college teachers in Canada taught her lessons which helped her to pay then and reap now. Throughout each experience, some things have changed while some things never change. Winggie is waiting to fly to the next off-ramp.

ABOUT THE AUTHOR

Gloria Smith was born in Saint Ann, Jamaica and immigrated to Canada in 1972. She takes great pleasure in helping people to grow personally and professionally. She loves to reach out to her community. During the COVID-19 pandemic, she participated in a church pilot project and delivered food to several families that live in Toronto and Peel. A mother of three children and four grandchildren, she has dedicated her life to raising them.

Gloria had a life-changing experience as a Youth Leader from 2015 to 2017, gaining patience, love, and appreciation for young people. One of her memorable successes is with a young man who had poor school attendance. Through teaching and disciplining, he is now a successful production manager. One day, he thanked Gloria by lifting her in the air and declared, "Thank you for being hard on me back then because it has made me into the man I am today."

She has been collecting socks for the homeless and The Centre for Addiction and Mental Health (CAMH) for the last five years. Her family, co-workers, and community members have assisted with donations of socks to the CAMH Suits Me Fine thrift store.

Winggie is Gloria's nickname from Saint Michael Primary School.
Facebook https://www.facebook.com/glo.smith.779/

CHAPTER 15

Little Miracles

by Leslie Burns

A muffled male voice whispering to another brought me out of deep, troubled sleep. 'If we don't get this right, these are the kind of people who'll come after you and your family.' I struggled to clear the cobwebs from my mind. What was I overhearing? Who was he talking to? Then like an avalanche, the truth came crashing down on me, through me, turning every inch of my being, cold. I could no longer turn a blind eye to what was happening. Years and years of anticipating the big deal that never came to fruition had culminated at this moment and I could no longer put off what I knew I had to do but had denied for so long.

It had been tumultuous between us for a long time. We rarely, if ever, saw eye to eye. Even the smallest of things like getting the kids to school on time or not letting them drink pop every day turned into an argument. The big things, like having goals and working together to achieve them, were always met with defensiveness, derision, and stonewalling. It was all common sense to me but having a partner who wasn't on the same page about anything was beyond frustrating and over time undermined my self-confidence and self-esteem. I grew more and more nervous feeling like everything was up to me. Life seemed a constant struggle. On the surface, we had it all, but underneath was delusion and denial. The dream and reality were untenable.

The thought of selling our home and ending a 19-year marriage was gut-wrenching. I had struggled against it for years praying and hoping things would get better. There was always the promise of 'not too much longer, the money is coming,' 'the big deal is coming,' but it never did. This latest development was too much. These 'deals' could potentially threaten our safety. I knew I had to act but there was one thing holding me back.

For years my world had been getting smaller and smaller. It was little things at first. I had always been self-conscious but I could squelch those feelings and push on. Then at work, I became more and more insecure about my job, my hands would shake, and I'd feel sick before going into a client meeting. Performance anxiety they called it. I felt like an imposter. The simple act of having friends for dinner would incite tension, anxiety, and defensiveness. The fear of being judged and criticized grew and grew until it became unmanageable. Walking into a group of people had never been comfortable, but suddenly, it became something to dread. My heart would pound, my palms got sweaty, and my brain got foggy whenever I had to be with people, whether it was family, friends, or colleagues. The voice in my head was a constant reminder that I wasn't good enough, didn't measure up, that everyone and I mean everyone, was better than me.

Everywhere I looked there were constant reminders to prove it. It became harder to leave the house until eventually, taking the kids to school and shopping for groceries was all I could manage. I couldn't understand how a once intelligent, creative woman — someone who had bought her own home and gave birth to two children — who was respected in her field, had earned a six-figure income for one of Canada's largest Fortune 500 Tech companies, could find herself scraping by financially, had become depressed, anxious, and for a while, afraid to leave her house.

I felt I was in limbo, afraid to stay and afraid to leave, but this latest development was too much. I had to act.

We left a difficult situation with very little. We left the place we had called home for 19 years and watched our family unit crumble. That year we were homeless for a short while, my eldest son left for school in the fall, and shortly afterwards, our sweet dog of 13½ years passed away. Nothing could have prepared me for the emptiness and level of heartache all this would cause.

Picking up the pieces and moving on wasn't easy. With anxiety and depression ever-present in my life, there were days it was hard to function, but providing a firm foundation, a sense of home and stability for my two boys, to see them educated and successfully launched into life, was more important to me now than ever before.

We found a small place to call home and I started selling more real estate. As the sole financial support for our family, I took on another job to fill in the blanks until I raised my sales volumes. I was constantly searching for ways to manage the anxiety I lived with daily, and just when I thought things were getting better, the unthinkable happened.

One sunny April afternoon, my youngest son, Ben, walked over to the optometrist's office to get a new pair of glasses, having lost his, a week before. I kept waiting for the text with a picture of his new frames but didn't hear from him. Several hours later, he texted to say I needed to call the doctor. She took several hours to exam Ben, only to confirm she had found pigmentation around the retina in his eyes. I held my breath, waiting for her to explain what that meant. She told me my son was losing his vision. I was in shock. My heart began to pound loudly and I had difficulty breathing. How could this be? He was only 18, just finishing high school and starting university in the fall.

By October of that year, Ben was declared legally blind, as less than 5% of his vision remained. Eye specialist after eye specialist, six in total, couldn't understand why a healthy 18-year-old would lose his vision, and so rapidly. They ruled out tumours, cancer, and genetics. With no firm medical diagnosis and therefore no treatment plan, there was nothing they could do. However, as grace would have it, one evening, my brother's dinner companion was a nurse. As he told her about his nephew's eye condition, she said it sounded like an ailment her sister-in-law had and told him about a specialist in the United States she was seeing. This doctor was one of three people in North America who specialized in acupuncture treatments that were helping people with vision loss maintain and even improve their vision at times. It wasn't a cure, but if we could help Ben keep the vision he had or give him a few more years of sight, it would be worth it! I did the research and was ready to take him but there were two problems. Dr Rosenfarb was booked months in advance and I couldn't afford to get Ben there, let alone pay for the two weeks of treatments.

Given Ben's age and the rapid rate of his vision loss, Dr Rosenfarb made immediate space for him. With the help of family, friends, and total strangers who helped through a GoFundMe page, fundraiser and a borrowed van, we packed up and headed for Westfield, New Jersey, not knowing what the outcome would be. All we knew was we had to try.

Our lives now look very different from what they did that fateful day six years ago when we said goodbye to everything we had known as a family, and to the life I had worked so hard for my entire life.

My eldest son, Nathan, earned his Honours, Bachelor of Health Sciences with a Major in Kinesiology after four of the hardest years of his young life. He is returning to school soon to further his education. Ben decided to temporarily let go of his dream of a university degree while going through the long and at times arduous journey of medical appointments and learning to live with vision loss. His level of maturity and acceptance of the situation and the bravery with which he meets each challenge inspires me every day. At the writing of this story, he is one semester away from his diploma in Business Marketing from Seneca College. He plays Blind Hockey and Blind Baseball and has met the most incredible group of people through these sports. He calls them his second family. They are living proof that life can still be lived to its fullest, even with a visual impairment.

Since Ben's first round of specialized acupuncture treatments in the United States four years ago, his remaining vision has been maintained and even improved for a short while. He receives regular treatments locally now through a Toronto clinic, Avenue Acupuncture. Ryan Longenecker, the proprietor, has spent several years learning and studying this remarkable technique.

As for me, my life doesn't look like most people's I know at my age and stage in life. It's messy and imperfect, just like me.

Anxiety rears its ugly head from time to time, like when I'm being asked to write a chapter in a book of stories about 21 resilient women, but I've learned to respond to it differently. I'm no longer at its mercy. I treat it like an old friend, welcome it in, and do my best to understand what it's telling me. I can be much more resourceful and choose to move through it or adapt appropriately. I've learned to let go of the people and things that no longer work in my life. I realize it takes strength to do so; letting go is not a weakness.

I wish I could say some grand miracle brought Ben's vision back or a windfall made our lives less of a struggle but that wouldn't be true. Instead, there have been years of deliberate and steady progress, as I take each day as it comes, challenging myself when I'd rather stay in my comfort zone. That and staying reasonably positive, has brought me to a place of peace, happiness, and deep gratitude.

Even when life threatens to take us to our knees we can learn to recognize the seen and unseen forces present in our lives in the form of what I like to call little miracles. For me, the whisper to wake up and take action, Ben losing his glasses so that we found out about his vision loss before he had an accident, and the staggering kindness and generosity of friends and strangers who came to our aid in our time of need, are all examples of the little miracles at work in our lives if we're willing to see them. Acknowledging those little miracles and not just focusing on the negative, made me feel I wasn't alone; that some greater force was at work and it gave me the courage to go on.

While these years have been difficult, I can be grateful that I still have my son while other parents have had to say goodbye to theirs. I can do my best to be there for others as they were there for me.

There is often no easy way around the difficult things that life throws at us. There's no quick fix, pill, or spiritual bypass that will help us avoid whatever it is we're going through, although a little bit of wine helps sometimes. Only grit, determination, an open perspective, and above all, resilience, get us through.

ABOUT THE AUTHOR

Leslie Burns has held progressively responsible positions in the corporate world working with and for Fortune 500 companies delivering technology solutions to large call centre operations. Her last position in this field was as District Sales Manager for Nortel Networks. For the last 15 years, Leslie has had the privilege of helping families buy and sell their single largest asset, their home. She is currently enjoying being part of the Emergency Roadside and Workforce Management Teams at CAA.

Her greatest joy of all has been as a mom, chief cook and bottle washer to two amazing young men, Ben, 22, and Nate, 24. Together with their dog Rayne, they have lived in Aurora for 23 years.

Leslie takes pleasure in the simple things in life like walking the dog, a cup of tea on the front porch, and spending as much time as she can in nature. You will also find her cruising fundraising websites and newsfeeds, looking for people she can help.

http://www.linkedin.com/in/burnsleslie

CHAPTER 16

How I Found My Voice

by Sweta Regmi

I am not sure how I ended up where I am today. Could it be by chance? Or was it because I refused to be judged on my looks, persevered, worked hard at my career, and found the courage to speak up for myself?

Let me take you back to 20 years ago. I was born in one of the poorest countries in the world, known as Nepal. My days in high school were full of insecurity as a female. I used to be a nerd in high school, with big glasses, a boy's haircut, and I was anorexic. While everyone within my group was fully developed and wearing a bra, I used to stuff socks inside my sports bra because I was flat-chested. I wore two pairs of pants to hide my chicken legs. Once, I shared my secret with a close friend and she told her boyfriend, and then I got bullied. I will never forget the embarrassment and insecurity that I had for years and how hard I found it to trust anyone. I started to understand that insecurity never ends so I had to move on!

I bonded with a girl in Grade 12 and we kept in touch and became best friends. She used to joke about making me her aunt. One day, her 30-year-old uncle who was working in the United States, asked to arrange for a bride. My friend approached me and asked if I was interested in an arranged marriage. Although I was just 20 years old, she thought we were a good match. I took a chance, sent him a picture, and waited. Keep in mind, we had not spoken a single word to each other, and my parents didn't know. Only his family knew that he was coming back home to get married and they were supposed to find a bride. I was close with my mom, and after a few months, I told her that I was interested in this guy and I could see my bright future, ahead.

My best friend's uncle came to Nepal to get married. She invited me to chat casually with him at her home and that was the first time I met him. I was interviewed for 10 minutes in front of my friend, her mother, the groom's mother, and the groom. They asked me a couple of questions and said they would call my parents. I told my parents the same day, "Look, I like the guy and his family, and I am going to marry him, whether you like him or not." The look on my parents' faces was priceless. I told them to go talk to Prad the next day and my friend's family set up the time and chose the venue.

One week later, Prad and I got engaged and after 10 days we got married. We flew to America after a week. I'm not sure if it was my dream of America or Prad that made me take such a huge leap. I was already smitten by stories that my best friend told me about Prad before I even saw my future husband. Prad and I often bring it up and giggle. I have been happily married to my soulmate for 20 years and we have two beautiful kids, a 13-year-old boy, and an eight-year-old girl. One of the most calculative risks I ever took in my life was on a "guy." My best friend – now my niece – told me that her uncle was the most wonderful human being and she was right. I wouldn't be successful today without my biggest supporter and motivator, also known as my husband.

A few months after we arrived in America, my husband was laid off from his job and we moved to Canada. We sold everything and drove in our financed car, with a limited amount of cash, to Toronto. I received a job offer from the fast-food industry, my husband got a job at IBM, and we moved into a shared house where we shared the kitchen and living room with the owner and their two kids. I decided to work two jobs, one at a factory at night, and the other was opening a fast-food restaurant in the morning, to save for my college tuition. I took pride in the fact that I would pay for my tuition without any support or loan. I enrolled in college for Business Administration and continued to work part-time fully on commission in sales. After attending a career fair, I got a customer service job at a bank right after graduation. I worked hard, continued to learn, continued to be a top salesperson, and was promoted within a couple of years to a leadership role. We later sponsored our parents and my siblings so that they could come to Canada. It was exactly what I had envisioned 20 years before – a brighter future!

It took me a while to understand how to manage relationships within the corporate world. As English was my second language, I was often insecure because I was made fun of many times. Most of the time I felt like an outsider, trying to shine, but I wasn't recognized for my skills and achievements. I barely spoke up or challenged anyone. I remember a white, senior leader who would talk about my body and the tight skirt and high heels I wore. He even said that he hired me for my "hot body" and then later said he was only joking. The first time I spoke up, I went to him and told him that I didn't appreciate the comment. I second-guessed my calibre, and whenever I got picked for any major projects, I started to doubt that it was because of my brain. Later, I had a female boss who was hired externally, who made me realize my strengths. I was promoted and entrusted with the biggest project within the company to bring down the talk time on the phone by customer service agents which became successful. That was the day I knew, my brain was responsible for my success and not my tight skirts and high heels.

My employers created a new role for me after the success of that project. The new manager I reported to, was a miserable, middle-aged, divorced man. I wasn't a fan of his from day one but tried to support his vision. He was also part of the white boy's club within the company. My first boss, who initially hired me for leadership, never had issues with me as I never spoke up against him. My new boss was the best friend of my previous boss and whenever I started speaking up, I felt that he retaliated negatively. I wouldn't get invited to meetings or they wouldn't let me speak during meetings if I were invited. Later, my boss started taking credit for my work. I became a rebel and started speaking up in meetings. I began collaborating with a new group of leaders who were mixed race white, black and brown, external hires, chosen for their abilities. Finally, I learned leadership qualities that I'd never learned from the homegrown leaders who had been promoted internally, based on favouritism.

The new leadership team started to support and advocate for me. One day, I was chosen for a coaching project again to minimize the talk time for the call centre. The team in Ontario was excited to be part of the project whereas the team in New Brunswick gave me pushback and hard times. We did amazing in bringing down the talk time for the site in Ontario and not so well at New Brunswick. My boss along with the boy's club tried to use me as a scapegoat. I refused to take the blame and stood up for myself. This director who was once my boss called me and started swearing at me, and threatened to destroy my career. I was shaken but I went to my manager who was his best friend and said I would go to HR to report the bullying and harassment. The next day I left for a vacation, and although I came back relaxed, his harsh words still haunted me. I chose not to complain as I received an email from this bully with an apology. However, the retaliation continued by the boy's club and my manager. At this point, I was ready to quit or move to a different department.

The man who had once told me he hired me because of my "hot body" now came back to the department. He was part of the old boy's club too and my boss and the guy who threatened me were his best friends. I went straight to him and said, "Either fire me or lay me off because I can't work with your friends who continue to retaliate and bully me."

A few days later, I was working from home when I heard they let go of the new leadership team who were my tribe. The next day I received a call and was laid off within one minute over the phone. Later, I hired a lawyer and sued them for toxic culture, harassment, and bullying, and they settled.

After the layoff, without my title, I lost confidence and self-esteem. I wanted to do something meaningful by giving back although I had nothing to give back. I had partnered with the charity called Laxmi Pratisthanin Nepal a few years before by donating some money and fundraising to sponsor kids and build houses. I wanted to go see the houses they built and the kids we sponsored and even taught at school. I left my kids with my parents and booked a one-way ticket to travel back home to Nepal, to a mountain.

It was challenging to walk on uphill mountain trails for eight hours, without roads, given that I had never stepped into a gym in my life. However, I was motivated because of this new tribe of volunteers, and a girl I met and instantly bonded with. She was 10 years younger than me, a victim of depression, and had attempted suicide multiple times. She came to volunteer in the mountains to heal. That's when I knew that losing a job is nothing compared to losing one's life. We became travel buddies and hiked in villages and mountains, and even went to schools and raised awareness about sexual harassment and bullying. Being laid off was a blessing in disguise as we both healed by educating!

Once I returned to Canada, I was fully recharged. I thought a job search would be easy, but, without a job search strategy, my pride took a beating. So, I developed a job search funnel framework by focusing on effective networking and personal branding. I started to receive multiple offers for the jobs which weren't even posted. After a while, I received an offer for a leadership role within a major bank. I accepted this new job but deep inside, I wasn't satisfied. I didn't feel that I was making an impact and I felt lost because I didn't belong there at all.

On a Friday, I packed my bag and left. I took a couple of weeks to think it through and then resigned via email, without securing another job. I was finished with that corporate leadership role after 13 years.

On the side, I had been helping newcomers to Canada to find a job, for free, as a career coach. Since I was familiar with both the hiring process and a jobseeker's pain, I took a risk and decided to be an entrepreneur, and that is when Teachndo Career Consultancy, through which I share my funnel framework with job seekers, was officially launched.

I call myself an accidental entrepreneur. Reflecting on the past 20 years, I never thought my one calculative risk would be the start of a new beginning. We women have brains too, so don't let anyone make you feel any less than who you are.

Recently, I released a video of a Nepalese superstar turned producer, who reached out to me to ask if I was interested in being in a movie. He must have seen my YouTube channel. When I asked him why he reached out, he said I was pretty and beautiful and he wanted to be my "friend" on Facebook. I took offence and released the video on my Facebook when I heard that he had allegedly harassed a well-known female actress. In her defence, I went live and raised awareness of the #MeToo movement and shared my story about the corporate world. That video went viral on YouTube. The media house then contacted me for interviews, which I declined. I didn't speak up for publicity, I did it for women who needed to be heard and supported. Most people have applauded me for speaking up about #MeToo. Women are our allies, support one another instead of competing!

I will raise my son and daughter without treating them differently because of their gender. I was raised as girls shouldn't speak up or sit or dress a certain way or be soft-spoken. I have vowed to treat my kids equally. Gender equality starts at home with our family. If you want to be heard, speak up for yourself! I am not the same soft-spoken woman once I was because I found my voice.

ABOUT THE AUTHOR

 Sweta Regmi found writing in English extremely heart-wrenching years ago, however, to date, she has influenced thousands through her content writing. Sweta conquered her "ESL PHOBIA" on LinkedIn by writing every day and her content is now viewed globally by millions. Her organic followers grew to over 100k within a year because of her high-quality content. Sweta Regmi is the Founder and CEO at Teachndo Career Consultancy where she teaches Dos & Don'ts to job seekers. Sweta is an accomplished coach with 13 years of leadership experience, gained from an award-winning company in Canada. Sweta resigned from that leadership role to make an impact in the lives of others and to ease the difficulties job seekers often face. She pairs her hiring expertise from the corporate world with a deep understanding of what employers want.

Sweta has written nine e-books for job seekers through Teachndo. She is regularly invited to participate in top podcasts, webinars, leading media channels, and at colleges, as a guest speaker. Sweta also hosts a YouTube channel through Teachndo. youtube.com/c/Teachndo

Connect with Sweta:
www.linkedin.com/in/sweta-regmi
teachndo.com/

CHAPTER 17

Growing Through Menopause

by Shirley Chisholm

Amber Alert! I was sitting in my car in the parking lot of the Diagnostic Clinic, puzzled and confused. My first lifeline call was to my childhood best friend with whom I am free to share my joy, pain, sorrow, trials, and triumphs. As godmother to my eldest daughter, she has been the contact for my family's 'APB' (all-points bulletin) whether it be for personal, professional, or emotional issues over the years; a trusted friend and life-long member on my Personal Board of Directors known to my children as a "Safe Place." Her familiar chuckle and the cynical, "What did I miss?" invited the launch of another segment of a 'day in the dramatic life of Shirley.'

My most significant health crisis to this point had been full abdominal hysterectomy surgery, five years preceding this call, and my friend navigated that course with me. A year after the surgery, I held her hands through her laparoscopic hysterectomy. Coming to terms with this major surgery was very difficult for me and I had deferred it for almost ten years from the first recommendation by my family doctor. The proximate causes for this delay were two-fold: a fear of hospitals – 'nosocomephobia' and fear of surgical procedures – 'tomophobia'. Both these fears were a result of untreated childhood trauma.

I was only six or seven years old when my dad had stomach surgery. I was taken to see him in post-surgery recovery but the 1960s parenting manual did not include 'preparing your child for a first hospital visit' or 'reasons not to bring young children to visit parents in post-recovery surgery.' That hospital was in a big town and to my childhood eyes, buildings hovered like towers. The hospital stood as an imposing white brick wall of corridors and windows. On the inside, our shoes squeaked along long corridors with highly polished floors and despite the sterile atmosphere, there was an underlying odour of death. My little hands gripped my guardian tightly. We stopped in front of a room and I was ushered into an unfamiliar zone – a blur of poles, wires, and hoses were attached to my father who seemed helpless on that bed that was too tall for me to reach. Was he dead? I turned around and took flight screaming as fast as my wobbly legs would run. My guardian caught me at the end of the corridor, chided me and dragged me back to the room, reprimanding me for being a 'spoilt child.' This negative experience would have an indelible impact on the rest of my life.

I was first diagnosed with uterine fibroids in my late 20s as they were discovered during an ultrasound after a miscarriage. They were asymptomatic fibroids and did not contribute to the miscarriage, although they were an unwelcome guest I would host for many years. During my second pregnancy a few years later, the fibroids grew as the baby grew, and at 5'3" I felt as large as I was wide and constantly fielded queries about 'the twins.' My daughter was born weighing 7lbs 12 oz and unlike my first pregnancy, I would spend six years trying to shed the 'baby weight.' By then the fibroids were no longer asymptomatic. Then I found myself pregnant with my third child – surprise! It was during this last pregnancy that the fibroids grew most aggressively. Nonetheless, I had a full-term pregnancy and a beautiful baby girl who weighed 9lbs 4oz!

MENOPAUSE - ARE WE THERE YET?

At this point, my monthly period took much longer to return, and my menstrual cycle changed for the worse. Month-to-month, I felt like a storm followed by a hurricane.

Initially, my family doctor advised that there was a possibility that the fibroids would begin to shrink in a few years with perimenopause as my hormone levels dropped so I opted to wait. Five years later, as the complications became more acute, I requested a test for my hormone levels. My male OBGYN conveyed the results that my hormone levels were so high that, "If we were to plug you in, you would light up the city of Mississauga." I was not amused, and I was no longer willing to live with this discomfort.

By this time, the fibroids were pushing against my bladder, kidney, and stomach, restricting their efficacy. Ultrasounds confirmed five to eight uterine fibroids ranging in size from an egg to a grapefruit. My doctor recommended surgery based on my age (mid-forties) and the fact that I had no plans for more children.

MY TRIBE

Interestingly, around the same time, I found community with friends undergoing similar experiences. Those that had the laparoscopic hysterectomy were champions for the less invasive procedure and short recovery time. My mental conditioning process also included conversations with my siblings. I uncovered a history of uterine fibroids on the paternal side of our family. Almost every female had experienced some form of non-cancerous leiomyomas (uterine fibroids) and had either undergone a full hysterectomy (removal of uterus and cervix) or partial hysterectomy (removal of uterus leaving cervix intact). This information was pivotal to my final decision. I booked a consultation with the OBGYN.

However, I wasn't comfortable with the male OBGYN and requested to be referred to a female. I was pleased with the referral as Dr B was young, knowledgeable, and had great bedside manners. In the consultation, Dr B recommended the full hysterectomy advising that she would leave the ovaries unless and only if they were unhealthy. Retaining the ovaries would prevent me from early menopause as my hormone levels were still remarkably high. So, I agreed with her recommendations, said goodbye to my cervix and prayed for healthy ovaries!

How did I prepare for this major surgical procedure? Preparation for the surgery required emotional and spiritual conditioning. I engaged trusted 'Prayer Warriors' and a personal Prayer Team (PT) committed to being with me onsite in fasting and prayer the day of surgery. They were my threefold tribe. My best friend from elementary school, my close friend and confidante from my very first job out of high school, and another close friend and prayer partner whom I had known for over 15 years. My pre-op counselling was booked the day before the surgery at the hospital, which was also my last working day leading into six to eight weeks of post-surgery recovery.

THE BIG DAY

Fear of mortality replaced feelings of excitement and anticipation as I walked into the East Wing of the hospital. The long corridor was surprisingly empty, and I wondered if this area was specifically designated for pre-op patients. As I searched for the pre-op admissions desk, I rounded a corner and there was a nurse wheeling a bed with a body or somebody all covered up heading in my direction with poles, wires, hoses ... My heart raced, throat closed, legs wobbled, and I turned and fled.

Outside in the parking lot, choked up and shaking uncontrollably, I used a lifeline. I called my dear pastor friend who was also a PT member. He picked up and I just allowed the tears to flow. I'd had a panic attack triggered by phobia. Twenty minutes later, after a prayerful intervention, armed with good counsel and virtual handholding, I went back into the hospital to complete the pre-op preparation.

The two-hour surgery was scheduled to begin at 10:00 a.m. My PT and I huddled onsite before I was called in for preparation. Just before 10:00 a.m., the nurse checked in to advise that Dr B had encountered some complications in the surgery ahead of mine and would be delayed another hour or so. I received the information with an amazing sense of peace and calm.

Dr B appeared just after 2:00 p.m. I had been receiving periodic updates from the nurses and was told that my surgery would be pushed to 3:00 p.m. Dr B wanted to let me know that due to the unforeseen complications with the previous surgery, she didn't have enough time available to afford me the laparoscopic procedure but would revert to the abdominal 'bikini cut' and assured me she would keep it low and neat. The surgery was successful, and I woke up to the news that my ovaries were intact and healthy – whew!

MENOPAUSE MADNESS

Although I had been distracted by the dominance of the symptoms caused by uterine fibroids before surgery, in hindsight there were some signs of perimenopause. For me, the symptoms showed up as me locking my keys in my car three times in one day on my 40th birthday, mood changes, irritability, insomnia, or the day I went to work wearing two watches – oops! My daughter reminded me of once finding my watch and another time, my keys, in the refrigerator, while I frantically searched other areas of the house.

Within my community of friends were shared experiences of hot flashes, night sweats, thinning hair, loss of memory, mood swings, irritability, lack of libido, insomnia, weight gain, and adult acne. One friend was wearing a fracture cast – compliments of menopause. She had been walking on a beautiful day on a clear, flat surface with no obstructions when she found herself off-balance and fell and fractured her wrist. Another friend who was quite a social butterfly on the Go Train became so withdrawn, irritable and unpleasant, that fellow riders avoided her on the train while friends whispered, "She used to be so nice, what happened to her?" Men-o-Pause.

I remember sitting in a board meeting one day, chaired by a woman when suddenly, beads of sweat appeared on her forehead and began to drip down her face. She became visibly uncomfortable and I thought she might be ill. She continued the presentation, looked up and asked, "Who closed the doors?" creating an embarrassing silence in a male-dominated room. The door was wide open, and nothing had changed in the room. She went through a full five-minute menopause sweat in the middle of her presentation and it was awkward! She received my prayers every day thereafter for a short and swift transition through menopause.

AMBERT ALERT

Post-hysterectomy, I felt light and free. I was no longer walking around feeling pregnant and was shedding some weight with diet and exercise. I had regular appointments with my family doctor to correct the pre-surgery bladder and kidney issues, and an annual physical included a pelvic ultrasound to check the health of the ovaries.

Five years post-hysterectomy I made the lifeline call from the parking of the Diagnostic Clinic. "I've sent out an Amber Alert for my missing ovaries," I said to my friend and continued, "I just spent over an hour in the clinic undergoing a pelvic ultrasound for my ovaries."

After some time had elapsed, the technician, quite perplexed, asked, "Are you sure you still have your ovaries?" A thousand thoughts raced through my mind. "Of course, I have my ovaries, I had them checked here last year." She turned away and continued the transabdominal examination. More time elapsed. She seemed no less confused. She completed the exam and mumbled that I was good to get dressed and the doctor would receive my results in two business days. "Please check with your doctor," she replied, in response to my query as to the state of my ovaries.

In the interim, before I had phoned-a-friend, I had Googled 'what happens to the ovaries post-hysterectomy' and in those few minutes recognized a gap in my pre-surgery research. This was my 'AHA' degree, compliments of 'Google University.' In the pre-surgery consultation, Dr B had forgotten to explain that in removing the uterus, the ovaries would essentially be floating in the pelvic cavity. Over time and in the process of ageing, it is expected that ovaries will eventually shrink leading into natural menopause.

I completed the call with my friend with a promised update after the expected call from my doctor.

The follow-up appointment with my family doctor was anticlimactic. We had built a good rapport over the years and would often discuss business, politics, and family when time allowed. He was pleased with the results from my blood work and my cholesterol levels were getting back to normal. We chatted a bit about current politics and work. As we wrapped up, I asked about the results of the ultrasound. Unbothered and nonchalantly, he stated that at my age (early 50s), it was expected that I would be in menopause and that my ovaries had shrunk. He had no further explanation!

It was another two years before I would notice the thinning hair and subtle hot/cold flashes. Night sweats came later and were relatively mild compared to the experiences shared by my community of friends. One of the least pleasant side effects I have experienced is sporadic memory loss. I recognized that I could not rely on my once photographic memory and became reliant on detailed written notes. I recall leaving a yellow 'sticky note' with no information on my bedroom door, intended to remind me not to exit the room without doing or taking something. I forgot what that something was. A string on my finger did not trigger the intended reminder unless there was a coordinating note. To stave off the exhaustion caused by insomnia, I pivoted. I would go to sleep when I felt tired at 7:00 p.m. or 8:00 p.m. for a few hours, inevitably waking up in three to four hours. I did whatever work that needed to be done during the hours of midnight to 3:00 a.m. before falling asleep for another two to three hours and get up for my workday between 5:00 a.m. and 6:00 a.m. That helped me to balance insomnia that would normally keep me awake for five to six hours, consequently leaving me feeling exhausted during the day.

A friend shared that her journey through menopause has spanned 30 years. Her pre-menopause started in her 30s, menopause through her 40s, and post-menopause in her late 50s - 60s. The symptoms of menopause are not constant. Many have shared that the symptoms subsided for months up to a full year and then returned even stronger than before.

Amber Alert cancelled! The doctor has declared the ovaries disappeared due to natural causes.

I believe in answered prayers as my symptoms have been reasonably mediocre. The journey taught me the value of knowing your family history, so I now openly share my health history with my children. I started a 'Gratitude Jar' during this time, inspired by my pastor friend. I make notes of the things (big or small) for which I am grateful and drop them in my jar. I value the friendship of my tribe, my close friends, and those in the broader community who were willing to share their journey as well as providing tips and recommendations on the most recent 'best' naturopathic remedy for hot flashes.

I am just grateful.

ABOUT THE AUTHOR

Shirley Chisholm is a mother of three young adult women and a corporate 'working girl.' Her innate discernment and situational awareness are born from her faith and deep spirituality.

A widow at the age of 32 years old, she has clamoured through adversity and championed challenges to opportunities with an effervescent personality that belies her circumstances.

She is a passionate cheerleader and champion for the progress of Black women in corporate Canada. In 2007, she co-founded Ebony Women Insurance Network (EWIN), geared towards coaching, mentorship, networking and a safe place for conversations and the support of Black women. She was honoured as a Role Model by the Diversity Advancement Network in 2016.

Shirley resides with her family in the Greater Toronto Area, Canada.

CHAPTER 18

Finding Opportunity in Adversity

by Taranum Khan

My career life is filled with adventures to be documented in a memoir someday. Have you ever looked at some parts of your life and thought, "Perhaps it could make a good movie one day?" Allow me to share a specific career experience where I was made to feel inadequate – less than – and how it pulled me down to the breaking point and back!

After a couple of years in the same role, I had been feeling stuck. It was a repetitive cycle of work that I excelled at and enjoyed. Nevertheless, the supervisor never acknowledged my contributions or those of any other team member. It was laughable that they didn't know the current tools and technologies utilized by us yet had the privilege of evaluating and passing judgment on our work. Unfortunately, management was no better. They were interested in receiving the benefit of their staff's work but gave opportunities for advancement and recognition to a select few in their inner circle of friends.

Having put up with the bias for far too long, in a bold move, I took the bull by its horns and approached Human Resources. My skills were being underutilized and it was about time to set the record straight. I was clear in my position, "If no other suitable opportunities are presented, I'd rather move on."

Within a few days, I was asked to take on a new project which seemed like a win, only to find out soon after that it was an uphill battle. My emotions were constantly manipulated by my manager which impacted my self-esteem and made me second-guess my competence and efforts. Despite running the show single-handedly, achieving outstanding milestones for the program, and creating multiple augmenting opportunities for the organization, my work never got sincere acknowledgement.

The competition I faced was against a corrupt mindset that gave the presidency to personal friendship over competence. I went into the role knowing about the inequitable conditions, with the hope I could turn things around, but I should have known better than to put myself through that adverse experience. The excitement of accepting the role was short-lived and performing exceptionally did nothing to change the sleazy situation.

Within three days of accepting the new role, my previous manager asked me to put aside what I was doing and assigned work that they wanted to be done. I wouldn't have minded supporting them, however, their tone was not only filled with contempt, it was downright condescending. They made it seem like my time was worthless and I should have utilized it doing things that mattered. As I was easing into this new work situation, I didn't want to rock the boat. Have you ever felt stuck between a rock and a hard place? The financial implications of losing the job weighed me down. I had to stay practical and knew that the mortgage and bills would still have to be paid. Therefore, despite wanting to push back, I decided to bite my tongue and let that incident slide. That said, to ensure that it would not get repeated, I decided to bring it to the attention of the manager who both of us reported to.

Though the preferential relationship between my previous manager and the new manager was common knowledge, I could not have imagined the unprofessional response that awaited me. Upon sharing my concern with them, I was brushed off, told to focus on things in hand, and to not pay attention to trivial matters. The statement, "You know that the person you are speaking about is my friend," made my jaw drop. They had made their position crystal clear.

That was just the beginning of multiple incidents that followed, in line with their flawed stance. Throughout the year, on one hand, I exceeded the program deliverables, crushed timelines and outcomes, built stakeholder relationships, and brought visibility and recognition to the organization. On the other hand, my manager turned me down when it was time to provide a reference. I was taken aback but had to acknowledge that they were upfront about it.

Can you imagine a love-hate relationship? To me, it seemed just that! Throughout this time there was no end to mixed messaging, which kept me wound-up tight. While a certain task was in progress, I would be patted on the back, encouraged, and told how great I was doing. However, as soon as it was accomplished,

I was dismissed with undermining words such as "lack of initiative and leadership." It would take them no time to rate my work from "unbelievable" or "beyond expectation" to "not good enough, worrisome, and needing efforts."

Every single event meant sleepless nights filled with the thought, "If I just get this one right enough to make them happy, they will acknowledge my worth." I was proven wrong every time. Repeatedly, I saw them shine in the glory of success, which was clearly, the direct outcome of my efforts. Just the same, I continued to make progress with no clear outline of expectations, minimal direction, and limited support. It was interesting that other than the management, everyone including clients, stakeholders, and partnering colleagues were grateful for all I had contributed to the program.

I was stuck again, feeling frustrated and unappreciated. In all of this, agility in planning and organization, openness to learning, and adaptability were key in keeping me afloat. Have you ever taken in the delicious aroma of chunky green chilli peppers cooked to perfection in a bright red tomato sauce? I don't know about you, but just the thought of it makes my mouth water and puts a smile on my face. It's a pretty versatile dish which can be enjoyed in many variations. You could add to it potatoes or peas, cottage cheese or soya, egg or chicken, fish or meat, use it as a sandwich spread, pizza base, or have it with white rice, pulao, naan or roti! The point is that the tangy, sweet-sour, spicy, flavour-filled captivating colourfulness of this dish represents my versatility as a professional. Perseverance was fine but reflecting on my strengths and growth was past due.

As the end of my contract drew closer, people at work speculated about what was going to happen, as jobs are considered hard to come by. Some well-meaning colleagues encouraged me to request an extension from the employer, while others checked in and shared openings they thought would be suitable fits. This work brought me great satisfaction along with positive relationships with colleagues, but the management had been a disappointment.

Early on, I had been told that the program would be wrapped up with a celebratory event commemorating milestones. Accordingly, I prepared for it, but a few days before the planned date, the management put the brakes on it. Their decision was based on the funder not being able to attend and as a result, they would rather devote their energy to other important things. I felt differently. Many employees had contributed to the program and deserved to be recognized for their accomplishments. Regardless of the funder's appearance, I wholeheartedly prepared for the event and expected it to be conducted flawlessly.

On the day, representatives of the funder showed up right before the event started, to everyone's surprise. This left the manager frazzled, but thanks to preparedness, all proceedings flowed smoothly. The room was brimming with positive energy. One more time, the manager and the organization were shining in the spotlight. Everyone was happy.

At the very end, after impactful presentations, experience sharing, and testimonials, in front of a room full of participants, guests, families, delegates, and funders, the manager wrapped up by saying, "Taranum is ever so optimistic that she failed to report on the challenges faced during this time." They went on to give a rundown of all those challenges over the next few minutes, while guests in the room exchanged confused looks. It seemed like an afterthought and an attempt to get the last word in. But to me, it felt more like a slap in the face. The vote of thanks had been delivered and everyone was ready to enjoy refreshments. I plastered a smile on my face throughout the event, but anyone who knew me could tell I was far from happy and was fighting my emotions to stay professional. Deep down, I knew that this was the final straw! I had received yet another left-handed compliment and slap on the wrist for a positive attitude and doing my job well!

I continued to perform my role unwaveringly in the face of the hurtful adversity, while guests networked, enjoyed treats, and profusely congratulated us before making their way out of the celebration. A colleague came to me and asked, "How are you smiling? I cannot believe what just happened. Why would they make such insensitively ignominious comments?" I responded, "It's all good. When people act unprofessionally, they're only dealing with their insecurities." I had managed to keep my cool one last time, which was hard but gratifying.

I didn't cry at the time but on multiple occasions, caught myself choking on emotions. The memory of this emotional abuse endured and surfaced while I was writing this story, but my tears provided healing and closure. Facing this adversity made me carefully reflect on the kind of workplace culture and opportunities I would choose in the future. Staying focused on a growth mindset, surrounding myself with family, friends, and well-meaning people, and seeking advice from mentors, was instrumental in keeping my sanity. I am grateful for each relationship that supported me and helped me to endure this turbulent period. In my gut, I knew that something in me had shifted and things were about to change. The tipping point had been reached. I could no longer stay in my comfort zone and let others walk all over me. No way in hell was I going to compromise my self-respect. I never have and never will.

I am writing this story knowing full well that I am sharing situations from my life that were difficult and made me feel inadequate. On the flip side, those were the very events that brought into focus my capacity to overcome adversity. They allowed me to discover my strength and resilience. Life might seem perfect from the outside and yet, on the inside, we are fighting our own battles. If it is any consolation, my intent in sharing some of the challenges that came my way is to inspire, infuse hope, encourage you to step out of your comfort zone and embrace your true potential with courage. Take ownership of your career and do not let anyone tell you what can or cannot be done.

Embracing my strengths has been magical. Letting go of fears that held me back opened the door to a world of potential growth opportunities. I walked out of the organization and that "celebration" with my head held high on a Friday and started a new, better placed and well-paying position on the following Monday without their reference. This is a mere fraction of all I have achieved since then. I also walked away with my bridges intact. I still enjoy solid ties with the organization and am on good professional terms with the management. Although this experience was rough, I came out of it stronger.

In 2020, 'I AM' standing tall, 'I AM' true to myself, 'I AM' my own brand, and I continue to #MakeTheWay for others.

ABOUT THE AUTHOR

Taranum Khan, Ph.D., CCS, is an Award of Excellence winning Career Strategist. She educates professionals to optimize their network with confidence, and shine on social media. Taranum is recognized for her contributions to newcomer settlement in Canada. She is a best-selling author and speaker. Her passion is creating a positive impact on lives and she persistently challenges norms to #MakeTheWay. She strives to create a positive impact on the career and academic journey of the lives she touches, locally and globally. Taranum has contributed to multiple publications, podcasts, and interviews on job search and personal branding.

Taranum prides herself on balancing her professional life around her family and she is happiest when collaborating with her admirably ingenious sons. Every conversation with her is uplifting as she inverts the focus for you to rediscover the strengths within you. She believes in being limitless and leads her life without conforming to norms!

Twitter: http://twitter.com/TaranumNKhan
LinkedIn: http://ca.linkedin.com/in/taranumkhan
Facebook: http://www.facebook.com/Tara.TaranumKhan
Instagram: http://www.instagram.com/taranumkhan/

CHAPTER 19

To Behave as Her Inner Woman Prompts

by Jenny Okonkwo

The direction of travel for most of my adult life has been anything but a straight line. Nevertheless, I am happy to say that it has been shaped by a continuous process of awakening that has always given me a clear sense of direction. As the celebrity, Oprah Winfrey once remarked, "The biggest adventure you can ever take is to live the life of your dreams."

Consider: How do we pursue our dreams when facing conflicts and resistance from others on a different path? Often, it takes years of painful self-discovery at the intersection of understanding the true nature of our inner selves and living boldly.

This perspective was masterfully articulated by Nathaniel Hawthorne in his famous description of the Sculptor Harriet

Hosmer: "She was very peculiar, but she seemed to be her actual self, and nothing affected or made up; so that, for my part, I gave her full leave to wear what may suit her best and to behave as her inner woman prompts."

Beginning to Grow

Having started with a fiercely independent mindset just like Harriet Hosmer, I have come full circle by appreciating the greater possibilities for the collective versus the individual. I have seen how collaborative teamwork can make the seemingly impossible possible.

Being a driven individual, I have relentlessly put myself under intense pressure to perform. As the author, Ayn Rand famously said, "The question isn't who is going to let me; it's who is going to stop me."

However, as a maturing adult, I have become increasingly motivated by partnering with organizations within the community, nonprofit and private sectors working together in the area of workplace diversity and inclusion with a particular focus on women, youth and immigrant professionals, towards shared goals that ultimately can make a much bigger impact on society. In short, I have realized a valuable lesson of leadership: that wielding positive collective influence at least has the potential to be much more powerful than personal contribution.

Despite all this, no one would be more surprised to hear that I would grow up to become a woman of resilience than my younger self. Like many women, much of my 'inner toughness' is not innate, it has grown through handling challenges including misogyny and exclusion that have arisen throughout my life since childhood. However, I also choose to believe that desire and commitment are important ingredients too. The willingness to embrace adversity is a big part of becoming a woman of resilience as is growing a thicker skin. Surprisingly, some of those 'tranquillity tools' include prayer, fasting, and professional self-reflection that allow us to learn from the most painful experiences and ultimately become a stronger person because of them. This is not to say that from the very beginning, I wasn't trying hard to be an avid student or a budding entrepreneur, selling beauty products door-to-door and my sheer joy at helping my mother exceed all of the monthly sales targets of her side hustle! However, at some point, I began to understand that so much more was necessary to succeed than driving yourself to exhaustion through tireless effort and self-discipline. That realization was the starting point of how I became a woman of resilience. I then realized the value of building partnerships and finding allies and sponsors to open new doors.

Early Perspectives

Everyone admires different women of influence, perhaps even subconsciously, because these role models exhibit the same attributes, we aspire to. We appreciate that different styles of leadership are required to confront different challenges. Even the most powerful leadership figures can choose to make themselves small when that behavioural characteristic is necessary. I strongly believe that despite these many differences, resilience is a common attribute for role models from all walks of life. The understanding that self-awakening is a journey rather than a destination is

key. That is because resilience will always be necessary to overcome the different challenges that emerge throughout the personal development process.

My professional career began around the same time that John
Gray published the famous book Men Are from Mars, Women
Are from Venus. Although women see men and men see women
– very differently – the fundamental psychological differences
that the author describes persist to this day.

I enjoyed the rough and tumble nature of my career and studies
before becoming a mother. This is partly due to my driven nature. During this early phase of 'becoming me,' I began to observe gender differences more closely and to study people closely
in conflict. Also, I watched the efforts of women in the workplace
to 'code shift' into the masculine social mores of what can often
be a man's world. I started to appreciate the vital importance of
soft skills such as mentoring, sponsorship, role-modelling, and
leadership by example. These learning experiences were the beginning of my understanding that a robust support structure can
help to overcome individual career advancement struggles. From
a personal perspective, learning from our mistakes and realizing
that there is still a place for focusing on our appearance and use
of body language to gain power and position, is to our advantage.

Key Lessons

In late 2016 I founded an organization called Black Female Accountants Network (BFAN), a grassroots volunteer-led professional
women's network that has grown to over 1,300 members and taught
me a great deal about servant leadership. Many of the challenges

facing the network were not just bigger than one woman's ability to solve, they were bigger than one woman's mind to imagine. There have been key moments when my BFAN sisters have said that God told them to turn towards me and those moments helped me to overcome huge problems that strained my faith and caused deep anxiety. I recalled other female leaders who have woken up in the night and thought, "I just can't do this alone." For this reason, I have always believed that women must find innovative solutions to move forward in their lives. My biggest realization is the value that I can bring to others. I came to realize, having participated in many discussion forums, that self-confidence can be nurtured through active listening to others who share their experiences. For example, I vividly remember my husband being startled when the leader of our prenatal class explained that he should not consider nurturing as a power struggle with the child. I have also learned that a culture of trust and respect have to be established before everyone will feel comfortable with openly sharing their personal experiences and confronting their demons in a shared spirit of what can be brutal self-honesty.

Moving to Canada was a life-changing experience for me. As an 'immigrant' there were times when I felt like a fish out of water. Nothing prepared me for the scale of the move and the immediate loss of everything familiar. My biggest life lesson was that no amount of prior research can replace the lived experience. I had to quickly adapt to the alien concept of networking (in every aspect of my life). Learning to become unbreakable and to develop a 'shock absorber' forced me to accept the limitations of my ability to confront every challenge, inevitably bringing a more philosophical perspective to the future. Key to this breakthrough was the understanding that in the absence of a support structure I had to learn to rely upon others and more than that, to have trust in advice from strangers when I was unsure which decisions were best for our family.

As for many women, motherhood was a transformative moment for me that brought a new vulnerability, as well as opening the door to a series of opportunities. In my experience, the support of prenatal classes changes women's mindsets by getting parents to discuss new approaches towards dealing with a radically altered future. Bringing up two boys with my husband opened my mind to different perspectives on the struggle that women have, which is to balance the desire to self-actualize with the responsibilities of parenting. The early phase of motherhood can bring a greater sense of vulnerability, insecurity, and even failure, than the pregnancy itself. A significant lesson occurred through my son's rejection of breastfeeding, the understated problem of "failing to latch on" as it is politely known. Because this situation requires patience and calmness to settle the baby, getting frustrated is the least helpful reaction from a mother. The problem was only resolved by my husband returning to the hospital at 3:00 a.m. to plead with the nurses for some more cartons of pre-prepared milk.

In addition to returning to work, I discovered almost by accident, that giving back was a route to self-actualization. This was part of my growing appreciation that influence can be more powerful than direct contribution.

Full Awakening to a New Sense of Purpose

The result of those key lessons was that I became three women: a professional, a working mother, and a volunteer. This commitment is a massive personal challenge that calls for resilience in the face of competing time priorities, personal struggles, and self-motivation.

Another important lesson resulted because of my son's first term at school and what it taught me about the importance of a 360-degree perspective on every situation, particularly where you are personally invested in the outcome. He tearfully complained of bullying during sports events. I had intended to write to the school principal to complain but instead, my husband suggested he observe events first-hand. Surprisingly, it turned out that my son was putting in the hardest tackles!

I have re-focused on volunteering efforts, especially around education and professional community networks. Public speaking enabled me to become a skilled communicator, which I found to be critical when leading groups of volunteers, as a volunteer myself, to drive impactful social change.

This period of my adult life has been quite a journey, mostly positive, sometimes exhilarating and occasionally exceedingly difficult to manage. The life skills we develop enable us to become better prepared to tackle future challenges and personal conflicts. Through self-discovery, I found that human limitations to personal achievement can be overcome by championing a cause through professional volunteering with like-minded individuals.

Onwards and Upwards

Having to navigate these three significant life roles of mother, professional, and volunteer has brought me the benefits of increased self-awareness, improved leadership skills through empowerment and effective delegation, and helping others become better versions of themselves. Through these accomplishments and life experiences, I am proud to have had the opportunity to pay it forward and build a legacy for the next generation of women leaders from my community through the creation of BFAN, which is transforming lives, one member at a time as I write this story.

As a result of these life-changing experiences, I have developed a much better appreciation of the greater role that women can play in society. Women today are CEOs, leaders in all fields of science, technology, and education. At the same time, many of the same gender-based responsibilities of being a woman remain, requiring continuous adjustments in our day-to-day lives as we develop support structures and 'life hacks.'

ABOUT THE AUTHOR

 Jenny Okonkwo is a passionate advocate for the economic empowerment of women and workplace diversity and inclusion. She is an award-winning CPA, professional community builder, speaker, volunteer, and author.

Her advocacy work has been formally recognized by the Canadian Government (Omar Alghabra, now Parliamentary Secretary to the Prime Minister), The Diversity Advancement Network ("Role Model" Award presented by Marco Mendicino, now Minister of Immigration and Citizenship) CPA Ontario ("Be the Change") and Toronto Region Immigrant Employment Council for "Collaboration in Leadership."

As a member of the AICPA National Commission on Diversity and Inclusion, Jenny was recently invited to speak and act as Conference Chair at the very first AICPA-CIMA Global Women's Leadership Summit Europe. She has served as a former Ambassador Group member on the CPA Canada Women's Leadership Council.

Jenny is the founder of Black Female Accountants Network, an award-winning volunteer-led group with 1,300 members. She is also an MBA holder, Canadian CPA, Certified Corporate FP&A

professional and CIMA (Chartered Institute of Management Accountants, UK) Fellow.

LinkedIn: www.linkedin.com/in/jennyokonkwo
Twitter: www.twitter.com/jennyokonkwo

CHAPTER 20

Breaking the Barriers of Image and Perception:
How Basketball and Cutting My Hair Changed My Life
by Cassandra Edwards

This is the story of how a woman of Jamaican heritage, born and raised in Brampton, Ontario, found herself and became an advocate for black women and mental health therapy. One thing will be clear as this story unfolds, life is not a sequence of events where one moment has to happen before the next, but merely an understanding that life is a compilation of moments, both good and bad, that have allowed this woman to choose her path.

❖

From as early as I could remember, my mom would remind me that although we resided in Canada, as soon as I crossed the welcome mat at the front of our home every day after school, we were in Jamaica. Through our chores and cooking, to hand-washing clothes and hanging them on the line to catch the morning sun, my mom made sure we earned everything and knew the meaning of hard work.

I am grateful to my parents for their investment in my education. As I look back at those dreaded evenings when my father would ask me to recite my time tables at the age of five, or when my mother edited my essays to the point where there were no words left, my education came easy. The dedication and work ethic of my family changed my life. My dad worked two jobs, surviving with four hours of sleep each day, while my mother worked in manufacturing doing general duties, and tended to our home. Amanda, my older sister by five and a half years, was everything that I wanted to be. I wanted to be independent and not burden my parents, as I felt they worked hard enough. I decided that I didn't want to have loans or have my parents pay for school, and earned a scholarship to attend a school in New York. As a student-athlete, I applied for a joint B.A./M.S. program to start taking master's classes as an undergraduate to help pay for some of my courses. To complete my master's program, I worked as a graduate assistant for the Athletic Department, assisting football players and track and field athletes with academic advisement and career counselling.

Growing up, one thing was certain, the image of our family had to be perfect. We need not ever tell other people our business. From early on, it was ingrained in us that public perception was everything, and if you had an issue, you sucked it up and kept going. What did I have to worry about? Stress? What was depression? We came from a good family, ate the best Jamaican cuisine, had a roof over our heads, and parents that invested in our future. But was that enough? Why is it that most black women can relate to the same experience of being afraid to speak out about their needs, thoughts and feelings, in fear that they will be perceived as ungrateful? Was it that we all had the same childhood experience, or was this simply generational trauma amongst black Caribbean people? We were to be seen and not heard, not able to have or participate in important conversations, and unfortunately, we were left to figure out how to be confident black women in a cruel world where we were told that we acted weird, spoke "white", and had people want to obsessively touch our hair or ask why our butt was so big. It was in my adolescence that I learned to validate my own experience and this fueled my practice of being a support to other women in the black community.

Crinoline. Itch. Stiff. These are three words that explained every Sunday. Sundays were about dressing in your finest, wearing white socks with frills and buckled kitten heels. Our hair was adorned with ribbons, baubles and plastic clips, and oiled with Blue Magic hair sheen. Image was important. Forget first impressions, the third, fourth, and sixth had to be just as special. Perfecting our image began with our choice of clothing, having our hair done, and shining our elbows and knees with shea butter and Vaseline, but it was also about how we conducted ourselves – with pride, respectability and confidence. Image was not only about our physical appearance but how we presented ourselves as young women. As two young black girls sitting in the kitchen, my sister and I were told that there may be times in our lives where we would have to work twice as hard as our peers to get half the recognition – sometimes three times as hard – to get half the opportunities. We were told that the journey to anything worth having would be hard and required a strong sense of self. Oh, were they right! Never did I imagine that my largest barriers would be friends, teachers and coaches, but I still vividly hear my mother telling me to, "Be like a duck and let everything roll off your back."

Eat, sleep, breathe, play basketball. I will never forget the Amateur Athletic Union (AAU) practices in the summer of my junior year. If you arrived early, you played pickup at George Brown College with the younger team in a sweltering gym with no ventilation. However, the practice began with running to Casa Loma, running hills, then running back to the gym, with only five minutes to change our shoes. We competed in a three-hour practice with women all over the General Toronto Area and Quebec. These practices were hard and gruelling, and our coach had his own "10 commandments" and a low tolerance for frustration. I played AAU basketball for some of the best teams in Ontario and we travelled to the United States for exposure for college/university recruits.

For the regular season, I participated in rep basketball, with girls three years older than me who were among the best players in Ontario. This program provided players with the best opportunity to expose and showcase their talent. Rep basketball was open to everyone, but contingent upon try-outs. Athletics were my life. From a young age, I played soccer, football, volleyball, beach volleyball, softball, and track and field. I distinctly remember having my parents take time from work to be at every event. They were my ultimate supporters. My dad would sneak to my events on his lunch break, lean on the door, duck in, and disappear at the end of the game. My mom was always referred to as "team mom" as she memorized every child's name and was hoarse from cheering in the stands after every event. I distinctly remember racing in a cross country meet during a crisp October, counting the heads ahead of me to ensure that I qualified for the next round of competition, and hearing my name called faintly, off to my left. To my surprise, I saw my mother sprinting alongside me with a blanket, cheering my name, yelling, "Go! Go! Go! Go!" every step of the way. As I crossed the finish line, I remember being engulfed in my mother's arms.

During my freshman year of high school, I decided to focus on basketball, wearing the number 32 to commemorate the legacy my sister left. In 2017, our jersey was retired. Not only was that a first in our high school history, but we were also first to go to Division I for women's basketball at Notre Dame. Telling the story, it sounds glamourous, because I was fortunate enough to have committed to a university by my junior year. However, it placed a target on my back. People that I thought were friends, started to turn up their nose at me, declaring that everything in my whole life was handed to me, when in fact, I had to sacrifice my whole social life to get ahead. I never went to a party or birthday party and was ridiculed by church members to "put down the basketball." I never went to my spring formal and never had any admirers or a date for prom, because I was "one of the boys." Could they not see this was an opportunity to get ahead and experience the world?!

My parents made sacrifices beyond anything I could have ever asked for. They printed off MapQuest directions, following them with a flashlight in the night, to ensure we didn't miss our highway exit and travelled across Canada and to various states on the weekends. Flying on a plane and purchasing food at tournaments was not an option. My mom prepared food the night before or brought a skillet to cook in the hotel, permeating the hallways with the smell of ackee and saltfish. When my teammates went to the mall in between games, I napped in the car, as my mom hand-washed my jersey in the bathtub for the next game.

How could I not succeed with such amazing people by my side? It might have been because of the politics that existed within the sports community, favouring certain families that had more money and more access to facilities and resources, or coaches who stated that I wouldn't amount to much and was not "crafty" enough to finish around the rim. There always seemed to be an obstacle in my way, whether it was competing with my teammates for playing time in front of scouts, or coaches who didn't believe in my potential; teachers who always had to check my work for plagiarism, or simply having to fight the perils that came with being black. Little did I know that my grit, resiliency, work ethic, and upbringing would be the deciding factors that granted me a scholarship. Basketball was not only a way of life but more importantly, it was a vehicle.

It was in my senior year of university that I discovered the importance of having realistic expectations for myself and others, and the power of perspective. I had to re-evaluate the expectations I had for people I cared about and look outside of their potential and how I thought they should act, and appreciate them, flaws and all. If only I had learned this sooner, maybe I would have saved myself from stress, disappointment, nights of tears, and heartbreak, but it taught me to be compassionate, assertive and allowed me to create a space for myself in times when I have felt like an imposter. This is something that I now encourage my clients to do.

The life-changing moment for me was when I sat across from my reflection on Central Avenue and took a good, long look. I went into a salon to get a trim, but before I knew it, I said, "Cut it off." Instantly, I was flooded with images and scenarios of people asking me if I had had a mental breakdown; if I'd lost my mind. Regret and shame surfaced, and for a split second, I was wrapped up in what others would think, what their perception of me would be. However, I had to listen to my voice and I was ready. I shaved my head. The process of cutting one's hair is freeing, a literal shedding of one's past self. As my hair fell to the ground, so did my fear of the future. I was now excited about my future. It was at that moment that I became a new woman. I felt confident and ready to trust my instincts and give my fears to God without having to be validated by another.

And so, I set off on the path to becoming a licensed mental health counsellor. Keeping my image intact often led to sacrificing my values and boundaries because I felt as though I had to compete with others to be proud of my accomplishments. However, as of this moment, I never looked back and realized that all of my life's journeys were preparing me for a purpose, and that was to be a voice and support for people who felt alone and needed validation that their feelings are relevant, meaningful, and deserve to be heard. I want to be able to give the gift of self-compassion. By God's grace, my journey is not done, but only just beginning.

ABOUT THE AUTHOR

Cassandra Edwards is of Jamaican heritage. She was an Ontario Scholar, obtaining a full-athletic scholarship garnering four America-East Conference Championships, and four appearances in the NCAA tournament. Cassandra went on to graduate with a Bachelor of Arts in Psychology and Criminal Justice, and a Master of Science in Mental Health Counseling from the University at Albany, State University of New York, earning honourable distinctions and Summa Cum Laude.

Cassandra currently works in Maryland as a clinical psychotherapist with various populations, providing services to those who have experienced depression, anxiety, anger issues, substance abuse, eating disorders, family and marital concerns, trauma, and other pervasive mental health conditions.

Cassandra creates a safe and collaborative experience for clients, believing that they are experts on their lives. She uses cultural experiences to tailor her approach for each client and recognizes the courage and humility that it takes to participate in therapy.

CHAPTER 21

Confidence Gives You Heels

by Evelyn Akselrod

Tuesdays were my wash days, and they were long and tiring. By the time I got to the last heavy blanket on this particular Tuesday, my white frilly top and colourful maxi skirt was as heavy and drenched as the blanket was. Fully worn out, I gathered my skirt to the side and made my way up the red concrete stairs, watching the watermarks made by my wet slippers quickly disappear from the hot surface.

As I entered the long hallway which led to the room that I shared with my little sister and cousin, I heard my grandfather's voice, "Come and meet a scholar like yourself." At 14, I had not been to school for four years. My parents were stuck in Canada trying to create a new home for our family, while my siblings and

I stayed with our grandparents. I looked ahead to the veranda where my grandfather sat on his large red recliner. My eyes were drawn to a handsome teenage boy who had a golden tan and the kindest eyes I had ever seen. He smiled and awaited my approach. I straightened my damp and wrinkled skirt, passed my hands over my sweaty face, and quickened my steps towards my grandfather. Conflicted by the excitement of meeting this cute boy and the embarrassment I felt knowing that I had to contradict my grandfather's false grandeur; I could not reconcile my feelings about this introduction. As he widened his smile, the young man asked, "So, what school do you attend?" Looking down at his light brown loafers and feeling three inches tall, I murmured, "Sorry, I don't go to school. Can I get you a cold drink?" As I quickly walked away, I couldn't help but feel completely betrayed by my grandfather.

I spent the rest of the evening hiding out at the back of the house until our guests left. While I wished I could have blasted my grandfather for putting me in that mortifying position, I never worked up the nerve to ask him why he did what he did. We never had a good relationship, my grandpa and I, and this newfound anger, hurt and utter humiliation just incensed me and distanced us further.

Thirty years later, even after his passing, I wish I could say that I understood him better, but I can't. I will never understand why he introduced me that way. The one thing that drained my confidence daily – was the one thing that he used to define me – and allowed others to do the same. Did he know what he was doing? Was this his way of dealing with his embarrassment for keeping me away from school? Could he imagine how belittling that introduction was for me? Could he have known that when

I finally got to Canada at 17, that my parents would have to beg me to go back to school because his voice kept ringing in my ears, reminding me that people my age were so much better and more accomplished than me, and I would always be less than? Or that the sheer sense of horror I felt by the idea of being 17 in Grade Nine would drive me to take every lunch, night, weekend, and summer course credit possible so that I could fast track my way to graduate high school? Did he know that his careless disregard and insensitivity would spur me on to study throughout the late nights and into the early mornings and I would end up receiving three awards on Graduation Day? Did he know that after seven years of not going to school, his words would repeat in a loop in my head and fuel me to complete a four-year diploma in two and a half years? Did he know that it would be exactly what I needed to change the trajectory of my life?

After I graduated high school and was getting ready to go off to university, my uncle visited, and sat on the stairs leading up to my room. In the coldest and most dismissive way, he asked my dad, why he was spending good money on sending me to school. "Don't you know that she will just go off and get married? How will that benefit you?" My dad winked at me and smiled, as if to say, *"Don't worry about what he says."* I stood there in silent fury for a few moments that felt like an hour, with heat building up in my chest, cheeks and ears. My mind was racing, recalling the words of my grandfather and all the things I wanted to say to him that evening on the veranda. Just then, my sister placed her strong and reassuring hands on my shoulder which sent a wave of cool confidence through my spine. With a calm and contented smirk crossing my face, I pushed passed him to ascend the stairs. I realized at that moment that I no longer had to care about the words of insecure and lesser men.

This, unfortunately, was not the first or second time that I was made to feel less than. "Girls are meant to be seen, not heard" was something that I frequently heard while growing up. The way boys and men sometimes said the word 'girl' was as if with absolute disgust. "What's wrong with you G-I-R-L?" This made me think that being a girl was completely intolerable. For a long time, I hated being a girl. I associated boys with being free, brave, strong, capable, powerful, right, deserving, and I saw the opposite in me. Unfortunately, this narrative turned a brave, fun-loving, confident little girl, into a shy person who hesitated and second-guessed herself. Because I felt this way, I wanted to make sure that other girls did not. I encouraged my little sister to be as bold as she could be. I wanted her to ride bikes with the boys, play outside and be independent. I helped her with her homework so no one could threaten to stop her from attending school. I'm sure I didn't protect her from everything, but I was proudest when I saw her growing up to be brave, smart, and assertive. I still am.

It's true, growing up as a girl in the Caribbean wasn't easy. Unfortunately, growing up female, even in highly developed countries is challenging; we share different but similar hardships stemming from patriarchy. First, many people undervalue us, believe that we don't deserve the same opportunities as males, and then underestimate what we can do when we try.

I learned to use people's underestimation of me to fuel my way through patriarchy and to help me shape my choices. I decided that there were only two options: believe them or be brave and believe in me. I could either let them tell me who I was and what I was capable of, or I could hold my head high and stake a claim on my own life. I decided to look myself in the mirror, recognize the strength that only I could see, and begin living my life my way.

It was and continues to be a struggle to limit the impact of other people's opinions on my life. I would be lying if I didn't say that they influenced how I acted at school, in relationships, in my early career, and sometimes still hold sway in my subconscious. However, the more I intentionally focus on my strength, the more that influence fades into the background and I am only left with my choice – be brave and believe in me.

As I approached my 40th birthday, I identified some of the things I wanted to accomplish in my life. I always knew that I wanted to have an MBA, do consult work, and help women to reach their full potential. With no plans for future employment, I told my boss that I would be resigning from my management job after 12 years of being there. Maybe it was a midlife crisis, maybe it was a career itch that I needed to scratch, or maybe I was simply out of my mind, but I had a deep and visceral need to create my future. It was scary but that need to live life on my terms was stronger than my fear. I went back to school and completed my MBA, started a consulting firm, and launched the Women in Nonprofit Network; challenge accepted and achieved!

Those accomplishments were not easy, they came with their ups and downs, but I believe that the downs made the ups possible. Unfortunately, my story is not special or uncommon in any way. Other women have experienced far worse adversities and have overcome them triumphantly. You may be dealing with your own adversity right now, but what this and all the stories that the authors of this book share, is that adversity can be overcome with a strong belief in yourself, a tenacity that is unique to you, and perseverance that will make you a resilient woman.

What is resilience? Resilience comes from doing difficult things, pushing your way through tough times, and treasuring your battle scars because they remind you of how strong you are. It's about the mindset that you develop as you face hardships and how you choose to respond to life's upheavals. Some of us decide to hold on to the challenges we have experienced and build our identities around them. Others decide that they will not give one more ounce of their power away to that narrative and choose to define their own stories. That doesn't mean that we should go through our circumstances alone. Help is available and we should seek it out. The act of seeking help in itself is a sign of great strength. Holding on to a negative experience, however, is equal to resigning ourselves to a life of unresolved anger, hurt and emotional torment. Holding on to this means that we are giving that person or incident control of, not only our past but also our present and our future, relegating us to small and fear-based lives. We owe it to ourselves to let go of things that no longer serve us well. We can either decide to let circumstances break us down or we can persevere towards a breakthrough; standing in the light of our power and potential, knowing that we are the only authors of our destinies.

Today, my motto is **Challenge Accepted**. When I feel stuck, I ask myself three questions:

1. What would I do if I weren't afraid?
2. What's the worst thing that can happen?
3. What would I want for my sister, niece, or daughter?

When the answers to those questions present an opportunity for me to be stronger than I was yesterday, I move forward with gusto and determination, because forward is the only path to personal growth, resilience, and self-confidence.

Many years later on my journey of personal growth, I visited my aunt who lived with us at my grandfather's house. After a few hours of a friendly catch-up, I was ready to leave. As I grabbed my car keys and kissed her goodbye, she said, "You have certainly grown much taller." I hugged her and whispered, "I guess confidence gives you heels." As the engine purred and propelled me forward, I saw my 14-year-old self in the rearview mirror, wearing a bright and satisfied smile that said, "I could not be more proud of you."

ABOUT THE AUTHOR

 Evelyn Akselrod is a Trinidadian-born Canadian who resides in Toronto, Ontario. She is a leader in the social sector and is committed to the economic security and inclusion of people from diverse and equity-seeking groups, with a special interest in supporting the advancement of women and girls. Evelyn believes in the power of collaborative and transformational leadership that inspires people to fulfil their unique potential.

Evelyn is the Founder of Altitude Management Consulting and the Women in Nonprofit Network. To fulfil her dreams, Evelyn made a mid-career transition and obtained her MBA in Leadership and Human Resources, along with her Project and Change Management Certifications. Evelyn currently works as an executive at a Nonprofit organization, supporting strategic development and public-private sector partnerships.

or a god who doesn't exist. As for me, I'm going to take and enjoy everything I can get my hands on. Now, say your prayers and go to sleep, and live the pitiful life you've chosen, you foolish girl."

"I'm not a fool," Winnie objected.

"We'll see...we'll see," Lucinda laughed, lying back down, turning onto her side, and closing her eyes.

Six

Seize the Day

Winnie always admired Lucinda, looking up to her, emulating her in everyway, whenever possible. Which was why, Lucinda's late night speech impressed her deeply. She took Lucinda's philosophy to heart. It was not a renouncing of God, per say. For there is no need to renounce what you don't believe exists. Winnie vowed to live for herself alone. All her old concepts of good and evil were swept away. From then on, anything that furthered her ambitions was good. Everything else was bad, something to be ignored, or crushed whenever possible.

After only a few weeks of adopting this new libertine philosophy, Winnie noticed a dramatic change in her life for the better. When once she had prayed to God for her needs, as Lucinda explained, this did not always bear fruit. Whereas, now, suddenly and mysteriously with nearly no effort, all of her wishes were made real.

Whenever she saw something she wanted, she stole it. When confronted with a house infraction, she lied, often placing the blame on one of the other girls. This made her very unpopular. Still, what did she care? She no longer needed or cared about anyone save for herself. In time, she even grew to mistrust Lucinda, and rightfully so.

Early one morning, Madame Charbonneau gathered Cora and the others in the parlor.

"I have an important announcement to make," Madame said. "One of our students is graduating. Lucinda has been purchased by a very wealthy gentleman, living right here in New Orleans."

All eyes turned to Lucinda, followed by a small polite applause.

"When are you leaving?" Winnie asked softly.

"Within the hour," Lucinda smiled.

It felt like the entire world collapsed on Winnie. Despite her new independence, Winnie feared losing Lucinda. It would truly be a lonely existence without her one friend, trusted or not.

Winnie watched from the upstairs window, as a most elegant carriage pulled up to the mansion. Two footmen loaded Lucinda's trunk atop. They held the carriage door for her. Winnie waved, hoping Lucinda would gaze up for one last good-bye. She entered the carriage, never looking back. Winnie watched them drive through the front gate and then out of view.

A month later, Lucinda returned for a visit. She came for dinner, sitting next to Cora at the head of the table. The visit was arranged by Madame Charbonneau. It was the perfect motivation for the others. Lucinda was a sight to behold. As finely dressed as they all were, it was nothing compared to what Lucinda wore. There were rings on her fingers, and pearls around her neck. Her hair was professionally styled. She looked like a princess, even outshining Madame.

After supper, Winnie got a chance to speak with Lucinda before she left.

"You…you look wonderful!" Winnie said in awe.

"You understand, now?" Lucinda asked. "I rose higher than any black woman could ever imagine possible. I have the best of everything. I give the man a few minutes of pleasure every few days, and he gives me my heart's desires. He treats me like a queen, even better than he does his wife. Follow your dream, take charge of your life, and put yourself before anyone else. You're the one who's going to die, when it's time for you to die. You are your own god. Carpe Diems…seize the day!"

****

It was not a long time later, Winnie and the others nearly forgot about Lucinda. Her name was seldom mentioned. That is until one day in class, before Cora entered the room, all the girls were whispering among themselves.

"What is it?" Winnie asked.

"You haven't heard?" one of them said. "Lucinda is dead!"

Winnie was speechless.

The girl continued, "She turned up pregnant. She tried to get rid of it. She bled to death."

"Quite! That's enough jabbering," Cora said, entering the room.

Winnie's mind was in a whirlwind of confusion. Was Lucinda's death the wrath of God, cutting the girl down for her wicked ways? Or was it all meant to be, and Lucinda should count herself lucky that she found some happiness in the world, even if it was for just a brief moment?

Seven

Jolene

Winnie enjoyed having the bedroom to herself, although she knew it would not last. She understood at some point a new girl would come, taking up the bed that was once Lucinda's. However, she never expected someone like Jolene.

Physically, Jolene was a perfect candidate to be a Fancy, young and beautiful. Inwardly, she was all wrong, the exact opposite of what Winnie had become. She went around quoting the Bible from memory, praying throughout the day, innocent, forgiving and honest to a fault. Surely, the girl wouldn't last very long, if not for the help of Winnie.

Against her better judgment and life philosophy, Winnie was drawn to Jolene, wanting to care for her as an older sister would for her younger sibling. Still, there were times; Jolene was determined to do things her own way, only to meet with the consequences of her actions.

So, Winnie set on the mission to enlighten her misguided little sister.

Late one night, as the two lie in the dark on their beds, Winnie whispered across the room to Jolene. It was the same speech she received from Lucinda, nearly word for word, for it was written in her heart.

When she finished, she felt good within, believing she had made another convert to the true path in life. She'd saved her little sister from the shortcomings and pitfalls of the wicked world. Only, to her surprise and disappointment, Jolene was not moved, purposing a counter to each of Winnie's declarations.

Jolene spoke softly, gently with a slight tremor, as if she were on the verge of tears. Her words floated across the room to Winnie.

"Oh Winnie, you are so wrong. And the sad thing is that you know it. In your heart of hearts, you know what's right and true. You're just afraid. You should never be afraid. If everyone put themselves first before everyone else, we would all lose. There is right and wrong, and there is a loving God!"

"You don't know that for sure," Winnie snapped back.

"It doesn't matter, really," Jolene said to Winnie's surprise. "If you are right, and there are no morals, no right or wrong, no god, nothing after this life, when I die it will mean nothing to me. If there is nothing but this world, then I will lie in my grave, not wishing I'd lived my life differently, believing I've stolen from myself. I won't complain or feel slighted, because there is nothing. It won't matter, because nothing matters.

"But if I am right, then everything matters. And when you die, you are looking at an eternity of regret. Winnie, turn away from this foolishness! It is never too late. God will forgive. As long as there is life, there is hope. Please, Winnie, reconsider. You are my treasured friend. Heaven won't be the same without you."

Now, Jolene was crying, heavily. Winnie's heart went out to her. She got out of her bed, walking across the room, sitting on the edge of Jolene's bed. Jolene sprang up into Winnie's arms, sobbing.

"There...there," Winnie whispered, holding Jolene close. "I'm sorry I upset you so. I promise I will at least think about it."

This seemed to relieve Jolene. Winnie tiptoed back to her bed. Staring up at the ceiling, she wished she hadn't promised to consider what Jolene told her. Now, the voices of Jolene and Lucinda were echoing in her mind.

****

It was all Winnie hoped and worked for. She was to graduate, to be sold as a mistress to a wealthy gentleman in New Orleans. She knew if she played her cards right all her dreams would come true.

Still, the battle of good and evil waged war within Winnie, though never did she dare to choose a side. Yet, it all came to a head, the last night at the school for Winnie, when Jolene asked her for a favor only a true friend, a sister, would consider.

Jolene confessed to Winnie she tried to escape. She told her how late one night, when everyone was asleep; she took one of the dining room chairs to the outside wall, trying to scale it. Sadly, she was too short, even leaping from the chair, to grasp the top of the wall.

"I can do it with your help," Jolene pleaded.

"Do you understand what you're asking?" Winnie told her. "If we're caught, it is the end of both of us. Unlike you, I finished with my studies, I stand to graduate. I'm already sold, and perhaps I can live a life worth living. One day, I will be a rich woman. So, if we're caught, that all gets taken from me."

"Then come with me," Jolene added.

"And what, throw the chance of a better life away so you and I can spend years on the run? When they catch us, and they will catch us, the best we could hope for is to be sold to a plantation, and spend the rest of our lives as slaves. They could kill us, you know?"

"You're already a slave," Jolene declared. "You're a slave to your sin. Come with me Winnie; trust in the Lord. He will save us and your soul."

"And where does this soul reside?" Winnie demanded, pointing to herself. "Where in this body is it? Can you show it to me?"

"It's more real than anything on this earth," Jolene proclaimed.

Winnie thought for a moment.

"All right, I'll help you on the condition you stop all this God-talk."

"I'll never stop praying for you, Winnie."

"Fine, just keep it to yourself."

****

Late that night, Winnie and Jolene crept from their room and down the stairs, keeping close to the wall to prevent the wood floor from creaking. They took one of the dining room chairs, stealing their way to the outdoors. Thankfully, the guards were at the front gate, none of them on the grounds. The wall was too high to scale, for one person, alone, that is.

Placing the chair against the wall, Winnie got up on the seat, her back braced against the wall. Jolene joined her.

"You ready? Winnie whispered.

"Wait, not yet," Jolene said.

"Having second thoughts?" Winnie asked.

"No," Jolene replied. "There's something I want to say."

"Not now, Jolene. We don't have the time for long good-byes. Just get over the wall and run."

"I want you to know how much this means to me. I want to tell you how much you mean to me."

"That's fine, now get over this wall."

"You are the sister I never had, and I love you."

Despite the danger, in spite of all that was at risk, regardless of loss, this stopped Winnie in her tracks. Jolene's words went straight to her heart like an arrow. It moved her to tears that anyone loved her. Never hearing the words before by anyone, including her mother, she'd long since believed it an impossibility.

"I love you, too," Winnie echoed.

In tears, the two women hugged good-bye.

"Shall we ever meet again?" Jolene asked.

"It's a big world, and I've known stranger things to happen," Winnie replied. "Besides, how many Fancy Girls can there be? Of course, we'll meet again. I'll be there when you least expect me. I'll turn up like a bad penny."

Winnie cupped her hands at her knees. Jolene placed her foot in the hand-cradle, holding tightly onto Winnie's shoulder, and then the wall.

"You ready?" Winnie asked. "On the count of three…one…two…three…push!"

Winnie thrust upward as Jolene leaped. Her fingers barely touched the top ledge of the wall. Unable to get a hold, Jolene fell backwards onto the ground.

"Are you all right?"

"I'm fine," Jolene responded.

"Quick, let's try again," Winnie said, reaching down to Jolene.

When they were back in position, Winnie gave the count.

"Again…one…two…three…"

With one tremendous effort by both of them, Jolene took hold of the top of the wall. Winnie continued to push. Inch by inch, Jolene shimmied up the side of the wall. Finally, she was able to bring one leg up. From there, she made her way onto the top of the wall.

Sitting on the edge, she stopped for a moment, looking down at Winnie.

"Are you sure you won't come with me?" Jolene asked one last time, reaching her hand down.

This was the moment of truth, time to make a decision, a life changing decision. It would have been easy to reach up, Jolene helping her over the wall. However, it was just as easy, if not easier, to go back to bed. Winnie was confused; both choices had their pros and cons.

"No, you go on without me," Winnie said, smiling.

"Are you sure?"

"Yes, I'm sure."

"I'll pray for you," Jolene said, her words falling down on Winnie like a gentle rain.

Jolene turned and jumped, landing on the ground.

"Are you all right?" Winnie called out.

"I'm fine," Jolene called back.

"Jolene…my sister…good luck…."

"Winnie…my sister…God bless you."

Winnie returned to the mansion; put the chair back to its place in the dining room. Slow, she made her way upstairs to her room.

Lying in her bed, she couldn't sleep. Her mind was racing. She would have to be on her wits in the morning. There would be many questions to answer, many lies to tell. Only, that was not the only thought that kept her awake. The voices of Lucinda and Jolene were battling in her mind. Winnie knew the debate would continue until she made a decision, choosing one over the other.